Zero**Theology**

Zero**Theology**

Escaping Belief through Catch-22s

JOHN TUCKER

CASCADE *Books* · Eugene, Oregon

ZERO THEOLOGY
Escaping Belief through Catch-22s

Cascade Books
An Imprint of Wipf and Stock Publishers
199 W. 8th Ave., Suite 3
Eugene, OR 97401

www.wipfandstock.com

PAPERBACK ISBN: 978-1-5326-7518-8
HARDCOVER ISBN: 978-1-5326-7519-5
EBOOK ISBN: 978-1-5326-7520-1

Cataloguing-in-Publication data:

Names: Tucker, John Houston, author.

Title: Zero theology : escaping belief through catch-22s / John Tucker.

Description: Eugene, OR : Cascade Books, 2019 | Includes bibliographical references and index.

Identifiers: ISBN 978-1-5326-7518-8 (paperback) | ISBN 978-1-5326-7519-5 (hardcover) | ISBN 978-1-5326-7520-1 (ebook)

Subjects: LCSH: Theology. | Wittgenstein Ludwig—1889-1951—Knowledge—Theology. | Philosophy and religion.

Classification: BR121.3 .T83 2019 (paperback) | BR121.3 .T83 (ebook)

Manufactured in the U.S.A.   07/02/19

To Linda, Aylee, and William

There was only one catch and that was Catch-22, which specified that a concern for one's own safety in the face of dangers that were real and immediate was the process of a rational mind. Orr was crazy and could be grounded. All he had to do was ask; and as soon as he did, he would no longer be crazy and would have to fly more missions. Orr would be crazy to fly more missions and sane if he didn't, but if he was sane he had to fly them. If he flew them he was crazy and didn't have to; but if he didn't want to he was sane and had to. Yossarian was moved very deeply by the absolute simplicity of this clause of Catch-22 and let out a respectful whistle.

"That's some catch, that Catch-22," he observed.

"It's the best there is," Doc Daneeka agreed.

—Joseph Heller, *Catch-22*

Contents

Preface

I have been trapped in the clichéd, superficial, proposition-based form of Christian religious life in North America for some time. I have also been familiar with Joseph Heller's *Catch-22* for many years, but it was not until a recent reading that I had an insight that provided me with a way out of this propositional, religious trap. The insight was that religious claims, as opposed to scientific or ethical claims, should be expressed only as Catch-22s because these paradoxes do not make straightforward claims about the world that can be believed or rejected. Catch-22s are a form of paradox that establishes conditions that cannot be escaped. Because of this, one cannot find hope in a Catch-22. This means that our only options are despair and transcendence. One cannot obtain freedom without risking despair. This is the only kind of risky invitation we should expect from any religious path that is worth living. As I reflected upon this insight, I realized that in some respects, common or traditional religious language has always used Catch-22s, though this has gone unnoticed. I persisted in an investigation whereby I translated theological claims into Catch-22s. I felt a freedom that comes when one realizes that the only way to escape a larger trap is through triggering a smaller trap. This paradox lies at the heart of *Zero Theology*.

I call this freedom *Zero Theology* because I make zero straightforward, comforting claims about the world. Another way of saying this is that *Zero Theology* makes zero theological claims about the world other than the ones that can be expressed as Catch-22s. In a *Zero Theology* world, people currently trapped in the identities of theists and atheists could converse as friends because their proposition-based disagreement would disappear. My goal is not to correctly align straightforward, comforting religious beliefs with some proposed metaphysical structure of the universe. My goal is to live a free and transcendent life. *Zero Theology* is not for everyone. It is only for those courageous enough to risk despair.

Introduction

In Western Christianity, there is a common preoccupation with the role belief plays in the life of faith. This is true even of ethical-based theologies because they appeal to religious beliefs as motivations for ethical actions. It is also true of Christians who emphasize relationship over belief, for while they claim that being religious is more than holding certain beliefs, they do consider those beliefs as basic requirements. After all, one cannot have a relationship with God if one does not believe that God exists. For most practicing Christians, a belief is an agreement with or trust in the truth of religious claims. These claims include that God created the world, that the world is lost in sin, that God has a redemptive plan, that prayer is a form of communication with the divine, that God will judge, and that we will be reunited with our loved ones after death. These are the framing propositions within which the various strands of Christianity exist. One may disagree with some or all of them, but that disagreement has to be articulated carefully if one wishes to retain the label of Christian. Outright rejection puts one into the nonbeliever or atheistic camp.

The central role belief plays in Christianity is revealed in the literal/metaphorical interpretive distinction that has dominated theological debate throughout Christian history, but especially since the Enlightenment. The modern commitment to belief participates in what is known as the correspondence theory of truth, which states that a claim is only true if it corresponds with or refers to something in the external world. Though it has been around for centuries, its ascendance to paradigmatic status during and since the Enlightenment has made it the presumed model of truth in the modern Western world. It works extremely well when testing scientific hypotheses, getting directions, making a shopping list, and so many other parts of human life that there is no denying its efficacy and power. But if having a referent is what it means for a word or sentence to be true then

1

religious claims can be true if and only if they also refer to or correspond with some external set of facts.

The literal/metaphorical debate is taken by those within the debate as being crucial to what it means to be Christian. Literalists insist that if scripture says "God is a father" then God is a father. This means that God is literally male in some way. The same literalism is assumed for other claims like "Jesus is the Son of God"; "Jesus was born of the Virgin Mary"; "Jesus died for the sins of the world"; and "God created the world in six days." For literalists, if these sentences do not correspond with something that is real, historical, or factual, they are false sentences. If one cannot believe that these sentences refer to the way things really are, one cannot claim to be a Christian. After all, if you do not believe "milk" corresponds with the carton in the refrigerator, you cannot shop for groceries. In extreme forms, literalists are religious fundamentalists or scientific atheists. They both agree that the criterion for truth is correspondence. They disagree on whether religious claims correspond with anything.

The metaphoricists, by contrast, suggest that religious claims are metaphorical approximations that reflect our limited understanding of the divine. They would say that the phrase "God is a father" is a metaphor utilized by a patriarchal culture that projected its own highest ideals upon God. Since the father was the most important and powerful person in the patriarchal world, it makes sense that patriarchal religion would declare that God is a father to us all. The same could be said of monarchical language. Since kings occupied positions of power, God would need to be a king with a throne, courtiers, messengers, and soldiers. The metaphoricists would point out that if we take such claims literally, we are not only betraying historical ignorance regarding concept formation, we are also guilty of idolatry because we are fixing God with human words. They see religious propositions as metaphorical expressions that reveal humanity's evolving understandings of the divine. Metaphoricists claim that literalists are idolaters, while literalists claim that metaphoricists are unbelievers in disguise. Metaphoricists regard literalists as undeveloped or immature. Literalists regard metaphoricists as unchristian. Metaphoricists include literalists as Christians when they value inclusivity and literalists exclude metaphoricists when they value conceptual clarity.

What is often missed by both parties, though only metaphoricists would care, is that both are worshiping the idol of the correspondence theory of truth. In a sense, they are both literalists. The literal literalists believe in a simple one-to-one correspondence between religious claim and objective fact. The literal metaphoricists believe that there is a correspondence between religious expressions and something objective, but they believe that humility should keep us from overidentifying those expressions as complete descriptions of God. In other words, literalists think their claims refer to facts in specific ways, while metaphoricists think their claims refer in general ways. Literalists believe that God can be adequately described. Metaphoricists believe God can only be inadequately described. They both think religious language is about referring or corresponding, and they both fear that if their language does not refer to something objectively real, it is meaningless.

I call the unquestioned influence of the correspondence theory of truth on religious language the belief paradigm because it controls and directs how we talk about religious life. Because it is paradigmatic, it is difficult to know how to express disagreement with it. Because we interpret ancient scriptures through its lens, we see it everywhere and think that the earliest religious adherents were believers in the same way that people are today. If I say that I do not agree with the belief paradigm, I will be heard to say that I do not believe in its religious claims, and we are right back to having the intra-paradigmatic discussion about literal versus metaphorical truth rather than the new discussion I am wanting to have.

This book is my attempt to start a discussion about religious life that escapes the belief paradigm. This makes it difficult to identify my intended audience. Almost everyone who might be interested in reading this inhabits the belief paradigm. Some who might read it are far more knowledgeable about the facts and concepts utilized in the belief paradigm than I am. There are those who know its history better than I. There are theological experts who have contemplated aspects of its conceptual life with a detail that I cannot hope to match. Such people will have an easy time dismissing my attempt to have a different conversation because they will categorize me with some prior discredited movement or skeptic who operated inside the belief paradigm. I can only say that I regard such experts with the same curiosity that I have for Sherlockians who play "The Game" where Holmes and Watson are treated as historical figures rather than literary creations. Such people know a great deal more about their subject than I do—except, perhaps, the single most important thing.

In the 1980s, my in-laws had a television that had a broken volume knob. The only way to turn the volume down was to turn the volume all the way up and endure a few seconds of extremely loud noise. Then, all of sudden, the volume would flip and go silent. You would hear it emerging from silence and begin to get louder and louder. If you missed your desired level, you had to repeat the process. That experience has stayed with me and informs this work in two ways. First, I want to flip you out of the belief paradigm that has dominated traditional Christianity into something new. To do that, I am going to have to turn the volume up to a ridiculous level. This means getting into some of the conceptual weeds that normally would be better left alone. The second way the broken volume knob informs this work is that I have come to believe that people hold to a strong religious conviction right up to the second that they do not. People stubbornly cling to their current positions even as pressure and anxiety make those positions difficult to hold. Internally, the change may be gradual or incremental, but externally, they appear to have undergone a sudden and radical shift. This sudden shift or flip gives me hope. This means that people who are the most vocal defenders of the belief paradigm today may suddenly flip into its most vocal detractors tomorrow. It means that you, my reader, who picked this book up as a member of the belief paradigm, may put it down as a member of a new paradigm.

To provide you with an example of the kind of shift or flip I am trying to bring about, I will use window glass as a model. The earliest forms of glass were colored. In their book *Glass: A World History*, Alan Macfarlane and Gerry Martin write about the impact glass has had on our understanding of the world and of ourselves. They write that while no one knows exactly when glass was discovered, the earliest examples that have been found were colored and used primarily "to glaze pottery, for jewelry and to make small containers."[1] Glass was regarded as ornamental or decorative. It existed to be seen. In those days, glass was looked at, not through. If someone had asked ancient Mesopotamians and Egyptians about the purpose of glass, they would have responded that it was a mysterious and magical thing that inspired wonder. It would not be until many centuries later that the Romans learned the technique of making clear glass that could be used in windows.[2]

Once clear and colored glass coexisted in history, the purpose of glass could be questioned. According to Macfarlane and Martin, between 1100

1. Macfarlane and Martin, *Glass*, 12.
2. Macfarlane and Martin, *Glass*, 15.

and 1700, glass began appearing in windows.[3] Colored or stained glass appeared in churches. Transparent or clear glass appeared in homes. I would suggest that this innocent development played a role in setting up what would become the conflict between religion and science. I do not claim that these two separate forms of glass were sufficient to cause the conflict but that they planted the seeds for the conflict that was to unfold. The conflict was over the true purpose of light, and each promoted a very different idea of what it meant to be enlightened.

The Benedictines were responsible for much of the idea that light shining through stained glass was a way of expressing the glory of God.[4] Referring to the relationship between the pictures that were presented on stained-glass windows and the light that illuminated them, Catherine Brisac notes that "since St. Augustine, light has been regarded as their indispensable complement, a vital element in their glorification, since God is also Light."[5] Stained-glass windows were connected to the earliest uses of glass. Superficially, they were decorative or ornamental. Because they were windows, however, they played a much more profound role. The windows were not only something to be looked at and appreciated, they also bathed the room and those in it in a different kind of light than was normally experienced in daylight. Anyone who has been in a room that is illuminated by stained-glass windows has experienced what makes that light different from the light that comes through a transparent window. The words that come to mind are religious words like *holy* or *sacred* or *reverential*. In other words, stained glass differs from transparent glass in that it is looked at rather than through, and the altered light that bathes the room changes the way you see yourself and others.

When transparent glass became stable and clear enough to be used in windows for homes, it changed the way people experienced home life. The window could become larger and could allow the person inside to view the world outside. A window appeared in a frame. The frame not only shaped the perception of those looking through it but it also shaped the way perspective was conceptualized by subsequent generations. Paintings are framed as though they are windows. In order to perfect his use of perspective, Vincent van Gogh made a frame that he would put on his easel so

3. Macfarlane and Martin, *Glass*, 20.

4. Macfarlane and Martin, *Glass*, 20.

5. Brisac, *Thousand Years of Stained Glass*, 7.

he could paint what he saw as though he were looking through a window.[6] The home, like the head, became the place of the inner and private world from which the outer and public world could be viewed. The windows were the eyes. They made it possible to receive light into the home while maintaining a protective barrier against unwanted intrusions. Transparent windows revolutionized human life. The development of transparent glass ultimately led to the development of scientific advancements. Transparent glass became the extension and magnification of the eye. The term *magnification*, like *enlightenment*, would now become more frequently associated with science than religion.

Language and glass are unique in that they are both instruments for and objects of human investigation. Poetry is akin to stained glass in that it expresses and creates by displaying its attributes. Descriptive prose is like clear glass in that it serves as a medium of representation or connection between the inner and the outer. It makes no more sense to accuse poetry of being failed prose because it does not represent the world than it does to accuse stained-glass windows of being failed transparent windows because they do not allow one to see the external world. Yet, that is exactly what has occurred. According to Brisac, "In England, the Reformation resulted in the loss of a great deal of stained glass, with an edict of Edward VI in 1547 decreeing that all monuments to Roman Catholicism were to be demolished."[7] I do not suggest that this was intentionally meant as condemnation of stained glass per se, but the Reformation's challenge to traditional authority and its belief that religious truth was available to the rational individual prepared the way for the Enlightenment's privileging of the power of clear glass over the power of stained glass. Scientific enlightenment was ascending while religious enlightenment was waning.

From the Enlightenment on, stained glass has been relegated to its decorative or ornamental role alone. It has had its capacity to enlighten robbed from it because transparent glass has become the paradigmatic exemplar of what a window is supposed to be and do. For modernity, a window is supposed to be clean and clear so that individuals looking through it can see the world as it really is. Modernity views any window that is colored or stained as a failed window. In a similar fashion, modernity views the beliefs of primitive peoples as superstitious or failed science. Modernity perceives stained windows as dirty windows that distort the world as it is

6. Naifeh and Smith, *Van Gogh*, 292.

7. Brisac, *Thousand Years of Stained Glass*, 131.

and thwart the only kind of understanding that it considers valuable. The word *stain* has moved from description to moral judgment.

The flip I am trying to get the reader to make is similar to trying to get people back to a time before the ascendency of the transparent-glass paradigm. This is impossible of course. I do not intend to demean the accomplishments of the clear-glass paradigm. I live within it and accept it joyfully. It has made the world smaller, cured disease, advanced understanding, and created the potential for more people to live comfortable lives. However, Christianity that tries to live in it tends to promote fundamentalism, liberal intellectualism, or scientific atheism because the clear-glass paradigm makes belief the essential ingredient in religious life. None of these options is very compelling to a growing number of thinking people. The transparent window provides a visual example of the correspondence theory of truth that undergirds the belief paradigm of Western Christianity. The stained-glass window provides a visual example of an alternative religious life that is not measured against clear-glass criteria.

The literalist thinks that religious claims can withstand the light of reason because they are true in the same sense as scientific truth. The metaphoricist thinks that since religious claims cannot be literally true in the clear-glass paradigm they must be metaphorically true and refer to something that lies outside all human paradigms. I want no part of either option. Instead, I want to be religious in a different way. This means revisiting religious claims and seeing how different they may be when approached in a different light.

In order to escape the belief paradigm, I am going to make some religious claims as Catch-22s. Making only paradoxical claims prevents the reader from too quickly entering into belief or disbelief, because it is not clear what belief or disbelief means when reacting to a Catch-22. The problem with the straightforward claims of literalists is that they are immediately susceptible to belief or doubt. This is because the literalist is at home in the belief paradigm. Literalists trust the correspondence theory completely. Metaphoricists, on the other hand, distrust the capacity of the correspondence theory they inhabit, though they think it is the only game in town. This distrust sets them at a disadvantage when trying to frame religious conversations with literalists. The metaphorical approach is always playing on the literalist's home turf. For metaphoricists, every theological debate is an away game.

The Catch-22s are meant to throw you off balance. I am trying to flip you out of the belief paradigm into something new. This new paradigm does not attempt straightforward theological answers for confronting the griefs of life. The Catch-22s make this fact explicit and encourage people to look to connecting relationships and fulfilling practices that are intrinsically rewarding rather than to instrumentalist beliefs or propositions that deceptively promise escape. Catch-22s are not like propositions that can be believed or doubted. They are paradoxical traps that can set us free. These traps require us to abandon the reasonable/unreasonable cage of the belief paradigm.

This book will consist of ten Catch-22s. Each catch will be put forward and then an expository section will follow. Some sections will read easily, while others will require more attention and patience. This is the way religious enlightenment works. It comes in fits and starts. It is freely given and only available to those who work at it. Prior to the Catch-22s, I will introduce the basic approach of *ZeroTheology* and the importance of confronting absolute grief.

What I ask of the reader is that you suspend criticism until the end. If you enter into this book already in defense of the belief paradigm you will only encounter positions with which you disagree or that you find nonsensical. I am not trying to convince you by arguing against belief-based propositions one at a time, although I will critique many belief-based propositions when they are relevant to a Catch-22. I am trying to lead you into a new room, a new sanctuary, and I will need you to close your eyes until we are all the way inside. We are coming into this sanctuary from the brightly lit clear-glass rooms of the scientific world. Our eyes, minds, and language will require time to adjust to the light of stained-glass windows. My hope is that once in the middle of the room you will see religious language and humanity in a different light than you ever have before.

ZeroTheology and Absolute Grief

There is a story from Hans Christian Andersen about a princess who arrived one night at a castle, seeking shelter from the storm. The queen of the castle welcomed her and, knowing that her son was in need of a bride, decided to conduct a test to see if the young woman was a real princess. If the young woman were a real princess, the queen's son, a real prince, could marry her. The queen placed a little pea on the bedstead and piled twenty mattresses on top of it. She then invited the young woman to sleep for the night. The next morning the queen asked the young woman how she had slept. The young woman said that she had not been able to sleep because something was in the bed that made her uncomfortable. The queen knew then that the woman was a real princess because only a real princess would be sensitive enough to feel the pea beneath all those mattresses.

Each of us lives on mattresses piled on top of a pea. Some of us try to ignore the pea. Some of us feel its presence more acutely than others. But it is there for all of us. That little pea has a name and its name is *grief*. Grief is how human beings respond to change, loss, or deprivation. Grief responds to and reflects two types of need. Circumstantial needs refer to the physical, relational, and emotional necessities of life. Losing or not having these necessities causes circumstantial grief. Absolute need refers to our existential or spiritual need to make peace with our mortality, vulnerability, and powerlessness. Absolute grief is what one experiences when one confronts absolute need. Anxiety is what one experiences when one tries to avoid it. Circumstantial grief can come as the result of human actions or it can come as the result of natural causes or accidental events. When caused by intentional human activity circumstantial griefs are injustices. When caused by unintentional human activity, natural events, or disasters, circumstantial griefs are heartbreaking. Absolute grief, on the other hand, arises from the existential angst over mortality, loneliness, and meaninglessness that all people are capable of experiencing, regardless of their circumstances. To put the distinction another way, circumstantial grief is over sufferings *within* life and absolute grief is over the suffering *about* life. Throughout this book, the distinction between circumstantial and absolute approaches to concepts will play a central role. These distinctions are based on Ludwig Wittgenstein's distinction between relative and absolute judgments of value.[1] I use the word *circumstantial* rather than *relative* because I think it better describes the nature of griefs that occur within life.

The mattresses in the story represent the ways we try to avoid or deny grief. They can be helpful, necessary buffers between human life and circumstantial griefs and they can be harmful, unnecessary denials between human life and absolute grief. Whether helpful or harmful, they are what must be subtracted to get to the pea, and the pea represents the grief that must be confronted in order to live a transcendent life. I call this confrontation with the pea *zero living*. One can only get to the top of transcendent living by going to the bottom of zero living. This process of subtraction also causes grief because it forces us to remove all the denial mattresses we use to avoid confrontation with the absolute grief that haunts human life. This process of subtraction and confrontation is what creates the possibility of religious living. I define the religious life as one that confronts absolute grief by continually deconstructing denial while choosing the transcendent responses of absolute courage, wonder, gratitude, and love.

Once religious life becomes possible, it becomes possible to choose or reject it. Both choosing and rejecting the religious life are intelligent decisions and the difference is not based upon any special knowledge that the religious believe that the nonreligious do not. This choice is also not based upon evidence that religious people accept but nonreligious people reject. For the religious choice to be free, it must be neither reasonable nor unreasonable, because each carries necessary conclusions. It must be non-reasonable. This is what separates the liberated religious or transcendent life from believers and unbelievers who are trapped in the belief paradigm. Both believers and unbelievers require that religious claims be presented as straightforward claims that can be judged as either reasonable or unreasonable. The belief paradigm dictates this requirement. The liberated religious, on the other hand, are content with Catch-22s because these non-reasonable paradoxes are the only kind of claims that can lead to transcendent

---

1. Wittgenstein, *Lecture on Ethics*, 44.

living. Catch-22s offer only the possibilities of despair or transcendence because they cannot be escaped.

The religious life described by *Zero Theology* can be found throughout scripture. It is in the many admonitions against idolatry found in the Hebrew Bible. It is also present in some of the Psalms, in rarely read Ecclesiastes, and in the frequently misunderstood book of Job. It can be found in many of the teachings of Jesus and in other parts of the New Testament as well. Examples from these scriptures will be given throughout this book. For now, it is enough to point out that it is glimpsed in Philippians 4:7, where the author describes the peace of faith as a "peace that passes understanding."[2] Though this peace is often taken out of context and cited by believers to justify beliefs that seem unreasonable, there is nothing in their beliefs or claims that transcends understanding. In fact, the faith they profess is all too understandable. It makes all the sense in the world to worship a god who will take care of you in this life and in the life to come. The kind of peace offered by *Zero Theology* transcends the understanding of believers and the reason of unbelievers. In this way, it is similar to Paul's claim that the gospel is "a stumbling block to Jews and foolishness to Gentiles."[3]

There are different ways of defining the little pea. How one defines the pea determines how one defines the mattresses. Though all mattresses have to be removed in order to confront the little pea, this does not mean that they are all negative or need to be removed permanently. While some of these mattresses are meant to shield us from circumstantial grief, all are meant to protect us from absolute grief. The two are linked. Each can make the other more likely. Each can make the other more devastating.

We could name the mattresses that shield us from circumstantial grief after Abraham Maslow's hierarchy of needs.[4] Every human being deserves these mattresses, from physical needs to security and love, to self-esteem and self-actualization. These mattresses are positive. These are worthy mattresses that have not been made available to all human beings. The unfair and unjust way these mattresses are distributed causes pain, suffering, and desperation. Impoverished and oppressed people, those who lack the necessary mattresses, live with constant reminders of the little pea. They sleep very close to it. The circumstantial grief of poor and oppressed people is not the kind of absolute grief that must be confronted and risked by taking the

2. Phil 4:7 NRSV.

3. 1 Cor 1:18 NRSV.

4. Maslow, *Motivation and Personality*, 15–30.

religious path of *ZeroTheology*. Of course, poor and oppressed people can also struggle with absolute grief, but that is because they, like the rest of us, are human beings.

Even the positive mattresses that separate people from circumstantial grief may become means by which people deny or avoid confrontation with absolute grief. In *ZeroTheology*, we are required to make the subtle distinction between the positive role a mattress plays in making human life bearable and the negative role the same mattress may play in preventing a direct confrontation with absolute grief. The easiest example may be the mattress named *money*. Money is neutral in that it can be used for positive and negative purposes. While it can remedy many circumstantial griefs, it is also the "root of all kinds of evil" because it is especially effective at separating people from the circumstantial griefs of the poor and preventing the empathy that could develop if those griefs were shared.[5] The role money plays in separating people from absolute grief depends on the individual. The despair that sometimes visits people of privilege usually accompanies the realization that as effective as money is at keeping some circumstantial griefs at bay, it is ineffective when it comes to guarding against absolute grief.

It may be the case that the more privileged one is, the more susceptible one becomes to absolute grief, because one has the luxury of too much free time. Correspondingly, the less privileged one is the less likely one is to give in to absolute grief. If this generalization is true, which I doubt, the ethical desire to alleviate the circumstantial grief of the less privileged may increase their susceptibility to absolute grief. Conversely, the ethical desire to have privileged people give up some of their privilege may increase their susceptibility to circumstantial grief while decreasing their susceptibility to absolute grief. Regardless, even the most privileged will deal with circumstantial grief, though it will be less pervasive and obvious. Whatever the relationship between privilege and circumstantial grief, absolute grief can be felt by people regardless of how high they sleep in the bed.

In a related way, we distance ourselves from absolute grief by focusing on demographic identifiers and the circumstantial deprivations that accompany them. We give our mattresses names that are important to who we are as human beings. These names may include one's class, gender identity, sexual identity, race, and ethnicity. We do not wear these identities over some generic concept of humanness. We are these identities all the way to

5. 1 Tim 6:10 NRSV.

the bone. Motivated by the ethical desire to remedy the unjust distribution of Maslow's hierarchy of needs, progressive and liberation theologies have reacted by putting all their energy into these particular identities, or particular mattresses, and the resulting circumstantial griefs.

Historically and contemporaneously, people in my identifying group have used these mattresses or identifiers to disempower and keep differing groups down. The white, heterosexual, middle-class, educated, Christian male mattress that I sleep on is further removed from more circumstantial griefs than the mattresses other groups sleep on, and this being on top has been the defining goal of my group. The empowerment that comes when people in these other identifying groups claim and define these identities as their own is important for both its defiance and its correction of inherited injustices. In our zeal, however, we sometimes think of these identifiers or mattresses as the mythic turtles that hold up the world. We think it is mattresses all the way down and forget that even though our identities go to the bone, we are all human beings who share enough with each other to participate in a form of life that makes communication possible. It is this shared form of life and the possibility of communication that accompanies it that makes our common threat possible. Mortality is not the name of our common threat, though it is the name of our common destiny. Our common threat, the little pea, is grief, and every human being is capable of feeling it regardless of how many mattresses separate us from it. While it is not unreasonable to think of ourselves as only our identifiers, it is not transcendent either. The traditional, theological name for seeing humanity as a single and interconnected species is *children of God*.

We could go another direction and name the mattresses after the seven deadly sins. Each mattress could name a sin: lust, gluttony, greed, sloth, wrath, envy, and pride. The modern mindset renames these sins as addictions, and they are the means by which desperate people try to distance themselves from grief. Promiscuity, overeating, materialism, escape, rage, comparative worth, and defensiveness are the seven deadly addictions of privileged, modern living. The removal of even one of these mattresses triggers grief and requires support groups, accountability, and willpower. The removal of all seven requires total withdrawal from or complete rethinking of privileged, modern life. As with most mattresses that we use to protect us from circumstantial grief, each of these sins has a positive side as well: desire, nourishment, incentive, rest, indignation, motivation, and self-esteem. When we remove these mattresses, we are only trying to determine whether we are relying on unhealthy addictions to avoid absolute grief or merely utilizing them in healthy ways to meet circumstantial needs.

Different people throughout history have struggled with knowing how to cope with grief. They have different names for that annoying, discomforting little pea. The Buddha named the pea *suffering*, and accepting it is the first of the Noble Truths. The other truths, including the Noble Eight-Fold Path, are designed to remove the mattresses that separate the disciple from the reality of suffering. Only in relinquishing the mattresses and surrendering the desire to immunize oneself can one find peace with the absolute suffering that accompanies the circumstantial sufferings of life.

René Descartes, perhaps the first philosopher of modernity, had a different name for grief and subsequently had different mattresses. For Descartes, the pea was named *doubt*, and it irritated him (though unlike the princess, he could sleep late). To deal with his doubt, Descartes surrendered to it by removing all knowledge claims that doubt haunted. These knowledge claims were his mattresses. His mattresses were named sensory experiences, memories, and testimonies of others. His ultimate recourse was to say that the only knowledge claim that doubt could not haunt was the claim that he, as a thinking self, existed. Even if he was deceived in every way by some malevolent and powerful spirit, there was at least a "he" or a mind that could be deceived.[6] Another way of saying it would be to say that the only thing Descartes was sure of was that he felt or perceived the pea named doubt. Of course, he then tried to put a new mattress named *certainty* on top of doubt. Unfortunately, Descartes's doubt has kept philosophers up, tossing and turning on Descartes's mattresses ever since (though Wittgenstein tried to get them to sleep on the floor).

Samuel Hopkins, the eighteenth-century New England Calvinist, named the pea disinterested benevolence and sought to remove every self-serving belief or practice that separated believers from it.[7] His mattresses focused on ideas like loving God in order to gain heavenly rewards or in order to avoid eternal punishments. Each is an example of loving God with a self-centered motive. While he held other religious views that modern people might find dubious or unhealthy, he was a staunch abolitionist, and I cannot help thinking that North American Christianity today would be better off if we heeded his admonitions to remove self-centeredness from religious life.

6. See Descartes, *Meditations on First Philosophy*.

7. See Hopkins, *The System of Doctrines*.

There are other examples that could be produced. The tendency to build protections between ourselves and vulnerability is natural. Most strategies call for making sure our protections are strong enough to keep grief at bay. The promise of wealth can deliver on removing some circumstantial griefs from life. Other protections or mattresses include security promises like a strong military or a good-paying job. The reasonability of these mattresses should not be denied, especially by people who already enjoy sleeping on them. However, none of these protections can deliver on the promise to protect human beings from the possibility of absolute grief.

The primary mattresses in the belief paradigm are religious beliefs. While they are usually mixed with the other types of mattresses I have listed, they are also a distinct set of tools meant to prevent the believer from confronting the possibility of absolute grief. In *ZeroTheology*, these beliefs are idols or forms of denial that prevent the believer from having the liberated religious experience that only comes from confronting absolute grief. By denying a confrontation with absolute grief, these beliefs also deny believers the opportunity of overcoming it with absolute courage, wonder, gratitude, and compassion. This avoidance feels like salvation to believers but their anxiety betrays their denial. Believers are anxious about their beliefs. This makes them defensive and controlling. The liberated religious life, on the other hand, produces courage, openness, and compassion. The strategy of *ZeroTheology* is to remove all pseudo-salvific mattresses that help us deny absolute grief so we can learn to live honestly and courageously with it. The zero in *ZeroTheology* refers to the number of comforting beliefs required for liberated religious living.

Another name for the little pea might be *the worst-case scenario*. The mattresses I would like for us to eliminate are all forms of denial that we use to immunize ourselves against the possibility of confronting the little pea because while it is our greatest fear, it is also our greatest source for authentic, creative, passionate, and ethical living. Because of this, I would like for theology to get out of the mattress-making business, out of the denial and avoidance strategies of belief. While theology should address the deprivations caused by the unjust distribution of circumstantial needs among differing groups, it must not neglect the necessary confrontation with the threat of absolute grief that unites us as a species.

The first step in a religious journey is to not take the first step.

If you want religious enlightenment, you *cannot* go searching for it. If you do not want religious enlightenment, you *will not* go searching for it. Religious enlightenment can only be found by those who will not seek it. You can only search for religious enlightenment after you have found it. If you find it after a search, you will discover that what you find is different from what you sought. If you find it after not searching for it, you will discover that you regret not having searched for it, even though you know that you would not have found what you were seeking.

Jesus says in Matthew 7:7–8 that if you seek, you will find. This is part of a series of wisdom sayings.[1] It is difficult to interpret. On one hand, it seems as if Jesus is referring to circumstantial needs. These are needs that we have in order to live. Just a few verses later he speaks of a parent who gives bread to the child who asks for it. Food is a circumstantial need. On the other hand, we all know that if this is what Jesus means, then Jesus is clearly wrong. People all over the world are asking and not receiving. Literalists will say that it is because they lack faith. They forget that suffering from lack of circumstantial needs is often a result of faithfulness rather than faithlessness. Job suffered greatly because he was faithful. Jesus suffered as well. Faith is not as simple as asking and receiving.

---

1. "Ask, and it will be given you; search, and you will find; knock, and the door will be opened for you. For everyone who asks receives, and everyone who searches finds, and for everyone who knocks, the door will be opened" (Matt 7:7–8 NRSV).

If Jesus was not talking about circumstantial needs that can be asked for and received, then he must have been speaking about absolute need, the need human beings have for meaning and peace amid the sufferings of life. If Jesus is speaking about absolute need, then the seeking, asking, knocking language he uses is not the kind of straightforward communication we normally associate with such words. The difference between expressing circumstantial needs and absolute need is not the difference between speaking literally and metaphorically. The difference is between speaking reasonably and non-reasonably. An absolute need is not like a circumstantial need, so we cannot use a circumstantial need as a model for it. In other words, seeking religious enlightenment is not like searching for normal and reasonable things.

Consider car keys as a normal and reasonable thing. If your car keys are missing you conduct a search. If you find your car keys, the search was successful, and if you do not, the search was in vain. If you see religious enlightenment as the same kind of thing as car keys, you are viewing it as a kind of normal and reasonable thing that meets a circumstantial need. Believers trapped in the belief paradigm consider religious enlightenment as normal and reasonable. They do not understand why unbelievers cannot see it for themselves. When Jesus says that if you seek you will find, I do not think he is guaranteeing that you will find religious enlightenment if you look hard enough. I think he is promising that the searching and the finding are one and the same. If religious enlightenment were like a circumstantial need, you could find it by searching for it. Since it is an absolute need, you do not find it by searching for it; you discover it in the searching kind of life. It is not something extra to be found. Circumstantial needs are about meeting needs *in* life. Absolute need is met only by *living a certain kind of* life.

The promise Jesus is making is that the search is its own reward. This is not something we say when we are searching for a circumstantial need. If you do not find your car keys, you will not say that the search was its own reward. The liberated religious engage in the religious life even if there is no guarantee of heaven and no God to make such a guarantee in the first place. They prefer the promise of the journey to a guaranteed destination. Of course, guaranteed results will always be popular with believers, whether we are talking about get-rich-quick schemes, a prosperity gospel, or an eternal heaven with loved ones.

The problem with guarantees is that they are completely dependent upon circumstances. They can only fulfill a circumstantial need. If the guarantee is not fulfilled, people waste their lives grasping at a circumstantial hope that is actually denial in disguise. Even if a guarantee is fulfilled and people get what they desire, they soon discover that what they have attained does not meet their absolute need. Nothing that satisfies a circumstantial need can satisfy absolute need. This is another way of saying that nothing that is guaranteed can serve as the fulfilment of a religious promise. If the circumstantial payoff only comes after death, then one is spending one's entire life on a search that may end up being in vain. Of course, the vanity of the search is not the issue. The issue is that when people spend their whole lives hoping to fulfill a circumstantial need, their lives are filled with anxiety and defensiveness about the beliefs upon which their hopes depend. They have to repeat the belief to themselves in order to quiet any possibility of doubt.

The most obvious belief that needs to be surrendered in order to transcend the First Catch is belief in the afterlife. This is because the religious search is its own reward rather than a guaranteed destination. For most believers, the motivation to choose faith is inextricably linked to belief in an afterlife. When we remove this mattress, we are not concerned with whether or not there is an afterlife; we are only concerned with whether or not we can live transcendently as long as such a belief remains a motivating factor for religious life.

The goal of removing this mattress is to help determine the importance this belief plays in a believer's life. If you live the religious life without believing in an afterlife, you are living the religious life without having a need or reason forced upon you. You are choosing to confront the absolute grief that comes from mortality with courage and compassion. This choice also removes a barrier between believers and unbelievers because the liberated religious are not making an evidential but inaccessible claim about life after death. Some believers will say that the religious life is defined by believing in an afterlife. This is the belief paradigm speaking through them. This is totally understandable. When the religious life is viewed in this way, it is a reaction against the fear of absolute grief. It makes all the sense in the world. It is not, however, a peace that passes understanding.

If you are a believer because you fear an afterlife in hell or desire an afterlife in heaven, then you are not free to choose the religious life. Since the religious life can only be entered into freely, those who fear hell or desire heaven cannot choose it. A believer's fear or desire creates a necessary belief that denies the possibility that death is final. This denial forces the believer to adopt a defensive stance against any scientific observation that calls the afterlife into question. More damagingly, it creates a need to justify the belief. Believers are always looking for anecdotal evidence that supports the possibility that individuals survive death. Using the strictest scientific or legal rules of evidence, there is zero evidence for the afterlife. However, this lack of evidence is not the point. My point is that if you can choose the religious life without believing in an afterlife you have a peace that passes understanding. You have a peace that is not dependent upon evidential claims, regardless of whatever evidentiary rules are followed by your community. This is one way the liberated religious escape the belief paradigm. Believers rest their beliefs on denying the finality of the grave because they cannot imagine living peacefully with the absolute grief risked by such acceptance. Belief in the afterlife is also one way of controlling people. Wherever right belief is the criterion for inclusion in a religious community and wrong belief is threatened with eternal punishment, one can be sure that honesty, vulnerability, and authenticity are inhibited.

When thinking about the worst-case scenario and the afterlife, one may be reminded of Blaise Pascal's famous wager. The wager says that since you do not know if Christianity's claims are true, you may as well live as if they are true because if Christianity's claims are false, then your death is the end, regardless of your belief. On the other hand, if Christianity's claims are true, and you lived as if they are false, you miss the rewards of heaven and get the punishments of hell. This kind of wager is the very definition of anxiety-based, threat-avoiding belief. Believers insist that the pea must be avoided, even if it means adopting an afterlife strategy that seems antithetical to authentic and selfless living.

Zero Theology is neither a wager nor a hypothetical rooted in anxiety. Like Pascal's wager, however, it is a strategy of sorts. Since you do not know that traditional Christianity's straightforward claims are true, you are better off living as if they are not true. If you can live courageously, compassionately, and peacefully while assuming Christianity's claims are false, then you lose nothing if they turn out to be false. If traditional theology's claims are true and God is vengeful, then the liberated religious want nothing to do with such a God and would prefer eternal judgment to eternal sycophancy. Using the First Catch as a replacement to the belief paradigm's insistence on the afterlife gets us out of believing or doubting and defeats the possibility of any kind of hypothetical wager. In *ZeroTheology*, the religious life is its own reward and is not subject to external rewards and punishments before or after death. There is no wager because we do not embrace the religious life in order to win. The traditional threats and promises do not touch us. The liberated religious life is a choice to live transcendently.

The conceptual problem with believing in hell is that it creates an impassable gulf between the believer and the authenticity of the belief. As long as hell is on the table, Samuel Hopkins's anxiety remains. How can you ever know that you love God if God decides your eternal fate? This question is impossible to answer through the introspective evaluation of one's motives. The possibility of an answer is undermined by the conceptual elements that afterlife belief entails. It is like the truth that one cannot live out a conviction if that conviction is required by law. For example, if divorce is illegal, your marriage of fifty years does not stand for anything and is not praiseworthy. Similarly, your choice to live religiously is not possible if living religiously is required to avoid hell and gain heaven. Believers cannot know if their love for God is genuine as long as they need to appease that God to avoid punishment and gain reward.

When a threat like hell is defined externally the solution is avoidance, and traditional theology offered avoidance through mattresses that promised eternal salvation. When the threat is internal like absolute grief, avoidance only makes matters worse. Any religious teaching that seeks to immunize us against absolute grief is denial, and as such is idolatrous. These immunizations come in theological explanations, reasons, and self-serving justifications. For liberated religious life to exist, would-be disciples must risk losing themselves to absolute grief by giving up belief-based faith. The only way religious life can tap into the power that comes from confronting absolute grief is to risk succumbing to it, which means letting go of our theological explanations or reasons and rooting out our self-serving justifications.

The First Catch is about a promise, not a guarantee. The promise offers an escape from the belief paradigm's demand for straightforward religious claims that can be believed or doubted. It promises the living of a life that will be its own reward. The promise is that seeking and finding are not two separate acts but a single united act that is only available to those who recognize that truth beforehand.

The religious need is only met when you no longer need it.

If you want or need religious belief, *you cannot have* the liberated religious life. If you lack belief, you *do not want* or need the liberated religious life. The liberated religious life can only be had by those who think that because they neither need nor want belief they are disqualified from living the liberated religious life. A person can choose the religious path as long as that person does not need belief. When you give a reason for having belief, you are expressing a need to have belief. If you need to have belief, you *have* to have belief, because it is a requirement. The second you express your need for belief, the liberated religious life becomes impossible. If you do not hold a religious belief, you do not need it and therefore cannot be persuaded to choose it. If you are persuaded that you need it, then what you have been persuaded you need is not the liberated religious life. Any reason that persuades you is a reason that leads to the idolatry of the belief paradigm.

When unbelievers give reasons for not choosing faith, they are doing one of two things. The first is a rejection and the second is simply a reasonable but alternative approach that is nonreligious. In the first approach, what they reject is what all liberated religious people reject: the religious claims made by believers. They find these claims unreasonable. Any reasons these unbelievers give for not choosing faith are reasons for not choosing idolatry. The reasons given by these unbelievers to justify not choosing idolatry are reasons with which liberated religious people agree. Since liberated religious people would agree with these unbelievers about reasons to not choose idolatry, those reasons are not related to the liberated religious life.

In the second approach, the reason unbelievers give for not being religious is that they are choosing the reasonable life over the liberated religious life. These are people who choose not to be religious because, having recognized that they do not need it, they choose not to pursue it. It would be more accurate to call them nonbelievers than unbelievers because they have not invested enough in religious belief to reject it. These nonbelievers are perfectly situated to choose the religious life, but choose not to for perfectly valid reasons. This is their right. As long as they choose to remain only reasonable, however, the transcendent life is not open to them. They do not regard this as something to be missed and would substitute *religious* for *transcendent* in describing what it is they have chosen not to pursue.

In order to get to the place where transcendent living is possible, we must first subtract the reasons people usually give for choosing faith. These reasons are idols. They come disguised as virtues or beliefs but they are actually self-serving justifications. One thing the transcendent life can never be is self-serving because to be self-serving makes total sense, is perfectly reasonable, and is therefore not transcendent. When people give the usual reasons for choosing faith it is because they are too interested in choosing faith. Of course, being too interested is the same as having a need to hold a belief and that is already a step down the reasonable/unreasonable path that leads to the idolatry of the belief paradigm.

Not needing to have faith means that one is never driven by the desire to be self-serving or self-protecting in the face of absolute grief. Absolute grief comes from the realization that no religious belief can deliver one from the pain of absolute need. Not needing to hold a belief means not needing to have a solution or destination that eliminates absolute need. Circumstantial griefs, on the other hand, are perfectly normal and arise when human beings are deprived of circumstantial needs. When one is facing poverty, violence, or oppression, one is completely justified in self-serving or self-protecting behavior. Such protection is part of Maslow's hierarchy of needs. It is reasonable and even ethical to protect in these ways. It is not an activity driven by the transcendent and liberated religious life, however. It is an activity driven by need.

It is not a bad thing to have a need. Human beings are defined in part by the needs we share. Because liberated religious living is the choice to live a transcendent life, the desire to avoid an honest confrontation with absolute need must be overcome. It can only be overcome when absolute need is accepted and when one confronts the absolute grief it triggers without looking to religious belief to make it go away. This is why the liberated, transcendent religious life cannot be attained by those who want or need religious belief in order to avoid the possibility of absolute grief.

Deep down, religious leaders know the risk of confronting absolute grief, which is why they play it safe. They know that if they expose people to the possibility of absolute grief they will lose some of them to it. People lost in absolute grief will not fill churches or offering plates. Worse, they may fall apart and give up on life. Success is also perilous. If people confront absolute grief and learn to live courageously and compassionately in its presence, they will cease to require the weekly grief immunizations given out by many churches under the guise of a hope that is really denial. They will not fill churches or offering plates if grief immunizations are all churches have to offer. Of course, avoiding absolute grief does not work either. When church leaders immunize people against the possibility of confronting absolute grief, they also immunize them against the possibility of real, ethical, authentic, and passionate living. People who are immunized against the possibility of confronting absolute grief are bored and boring, risk averse and petty, childish and possessive. They are infantile.

Churches have been infantilizing people to keep them in denial and in the pews. The fact that many congregants are addicted to their grief immunizations will keep them coming to churches and filling the offering plates until they die. In infantile congregations, clergy who need to be needed thrive, while clergy who want to transform lives battle depression and burn out. Clergy themselves reinforce this trap when they condescendingly see human beings as fundamentally weak rather than fundamentally strong. Even people struggling with "least of these" conditions that characterize circumstantial grief deserve the opportunity to confront absolute grief.[1] Not giving them that opportunity consigns them to an immunized and antiseptic life and leaves them unprepared for dealing with either circumstantial or absolute grief. No wonder people who want to live authentically and passionately have zero interest in church and zero interest in theology. Many religious leaders want to be passionate transformers, but their fear of losing those addicted to grief immunizations, their inability to overcome

---

1. Matt 25:31–46 NRSV. The dispute over whether the "least of these" includes people outside of the faith community is rendered irrelevant by other places where Jesus speaks of a neighbor Samaritan and loving one's enemies.

the belief paradigm, and their presumption that people are weak make this difficult or impossible for most.

I think it would be a beneficial exercise if all clergy and religious folk were to read influential acting teacher Constantin Stanislavsky's book *An Actor Prepares*, and translate what it teaches about acting into what it might teach about living vulnerably, authentically, and passionately. In one scene, the Director, who is teaching beginning actors, contrasts the disconnected or meaningless act of closing a door with the connected or meaningful act of closing a door. In the first instance, the actor rises, walks to the door and bangs it shut without concern for the role the action plays in the plot. The act of closing the door is regarded as incidental to the play. In the second instance, the Director creates an *as if* scenario where there is a madman escaped from the lunatic asylum in the next room. This time, the actor closes the door with urgency and intention because the act is motivated by something important and connected to the plot.[2] Adopting the imaginative *as if* is one way of breaking out of the belief paradigm.

In my opinion, much of progressive theology is like the original scenario where closing the door has no connection with a plot. Many progressive theologians abandoned the *if* scenario that said, "*if* judgment and hellfire await you beyond the door" and forgot to replace it with a new *as if* scenario to make religious life powerful. Progressives, who are still overreacting to the old threat of hell and the shaming tactics used by religious institutions to control, have produced a superficial and comfortable faith that is as thoughtless and powerless as the disconnected and incidental act of closing a door without contextual motivation. This superficial faith serves to muffle the little pea of absolute grief beneath layers of mattresses named after ethical, political, psychological, and pastoral concerns. By making theology only about ethics, progressives have forgotten that religious life is a response and that one of the main things it responds to is the existential threat of absolute grief. Where there is no existential threat, there is no context or connection to a plot that gives religious life authenticity, passion, and power.

Traditional believers have held onto the idea of threat, but fewer people are taking their plot seriously. The numbers of people who believe in hell are dwindling. The numbers of people who fear going there are even fewer. I am delighted that the threat of hell is losing its power. My fellow progressives deserve some credit for disempowering the threat of hell,

2 Stanislavsky, *An Actor Prepares*, 45–47.

though they had to take the metaphoricist path to do so. Unfortunately, they have also disempowered the idea of existential threat and, in so doing, have disempowered the potential of a religious response. The existential threat that faces all human beings, regardless of class, sexuality, gender, race, education, ethnicity, religion, or nationality, is the threat of absolute grief. It is the pea that all human beings are capable of perceiving beneath the distractions of life. The cost of rightly focusing on identity theologies and the problem of privilege is that we have tended to forget that we are one species with one common threat. This has blinded us to the possibility of confronting absolute grief. The legitimate and overdue concern about the circumstantial deprivations that the privileged have forced upon the non-privileged has kept us focused on ethical imperatives while separating us from the source that could convert those ethical imperatives into more effective compassionate connectedness. Ethical imperatives are most necessary in relationships that are not connected and least necessary in relationships that are connected. These ethical imperatives, both noble and necessary, would be strengthened if they were undergirded with the vulnerability, authenticity, and passion that comes from facing the absolute grief that haunts and connects all human life.

What we need is a new *as if* scenario. The greater the risk invited by the new *as if* scenario, the greater the power to connect and transform. The risk is despair. The reward is transcendence. This new *as if* scenario creates the context in which the actor's actions have meaning. Rather than the "*as if* judgment and hell are waiting for you beyond the door" of traditional theology or the "*as if* there are no consequences whether the door is opened or closed" of progressive theology, I propose the "*as if* the worst-case scenario is true" of *ZeroTheology*. When we play *as if the worst-case scenario is true* we are subtracting from our lives all those mattresses or beliefs that help us avoid the possibility of absolute grief. Much of what we think of as faith will be exposed as idolatry. Much of what generates disagreement between believers and unbelievers will be eliminated, creating the possibility of community where now there is a division over claims.

If we begin at the bottom, with that little pea, I would define the worst-case scenario as the possibility that life is purposeless, vulnerable, violent, finite, and forgettable. For most believers, this would be the worst thing imaginable. Entailed in this *as if the worst-case scenario is true* is the loss of any divine mind who knows us or cares about us. Included in this scenario is the assumption that the righteous will never be rewarded nor the wicked punished. The innocent who suffer will have no recourse. The perpetrators who inflict harm will face no justice. The rain will fall on the just and the unjust.[3] You will die and be forgotten. Our species will go extinct. Our poetry, music, art, religion, and science will amount to nothing. All human accomplishment is ultimately in vain.[4] This is what absolute grief looks like.

Circumstantial grief can make things even worse. You can be lonely and starving and poor. You can be sick, suffering, and dying. You can have no prospects for a better life. You can be completely bereft of circumstantial hope and still accept the worst-case scenario of absolute grief. This is *zero living*. Whether you accept this worst-case scenario or not, imagining it as the *as if* scenario is the only place from which you can freely choose to live the liberated religious life. Stopping short of *zero living* means stopping short of transcendent living. Stopping short of *zero living* means that you are on a mattress of denial, trying to avoid oblivion.

The possibility of having a peace that passes understanding is the driving force behind liberated religious living. It takes *zero living* to get there. If you can be at peace, even if the worst-case scenario is true, even if you have zero denial strategies and zero comforting beliefs, then you have a peace that trumps all others. Many people profess having peace as long as they are on a comfortable mattress, but if you can have peace with the pea known as grief, then your peace is unassailable and transcendent.

Living *as if* the worst-case scenario is true, and the call to confront absolute grief, is really the story of Job. The story of Job is actually a story of the removal of mattresses. In the opening chapters of Job, he loses the mattresses of possessions, status, favor, family, and health. He also loses the appearance of faithfulness since his friends regard his calamity as a sign of faithlessness on his part. All this because the Adversary had appeared to God and made the absolute grief argument that I have been making. The Adversary basically says, "As long as Job is sleeping on comfortable mattresses it is easy for him to have faith. Take away the mattresses and we will see what kind of faith Job really has."[5] The removal of these circumstantial needs prepares Job for his confrontation with his absolute need, and in the context of the book, Job's absolute need was to believe in a God who maintained moral order in the universe. What Job encounters in God is a deafening silence regarding that moral order. God refuses to satisfy, and

3. Matt 5:45 NRSV.

4. Eccl 1:2.

5. Job 1:9–11.

in that lack of satisfaction Job learns that he had, along with his friends, constructed an idol and called it divine. Unlike his friends, Job is able to live with that unsatisfying God. His friends persist in their idolatry throughout the book because they never dare to question their conception of God. *Zero Theology* embraces Job's confrontation with God in an attempt to achieve Job's peace, a peace that passed the understanding of his believing friends.

Third Catch

The only acceptable evidence for religious belief is evidence that is unacceptable.

If you have a religious belief, it is because you lack evidence. If you have evidence, then you lack the ability to have a religious belief. The liberated religious life eschews evidence because any evidence that confirms religious belief destroys the possibility of having religious belief. If you have evidence that justifies or confirms your religious belief, you do not have a religious belief, you have a knowledge claim. This is true regardless of whatever rules of evidence your community follows. If all the evidence that is required is the personal testimony of a relative, then that evidence stands as certain for you as evidence derived from experimental confirmation stands for a scientist. As long as religious living is defined as the holding of beliefs, religious life is forever trapped in the Third Catch. As soon as you have evidence, you lose belief. As long as you have belief, you lack evidence. Within the belief paradigm trap, a religious belief stands to what is believed as a scientific hypothesis stands to what is hypothesized. Unlike what is hypothesized, however, the belief paradigm maintains that there is still more evidence to consider when a particular belief seems to have been falsified. Religious belief should never be like a scientific hypothesis, which is to say that religious belief should not really be *belief* at all.

One problem with belief in the belief paradigm is that God never fully reveals Godself and will not until the end of time. The end of time is the end of faith. In the famous passage from 1 Corinthians, Paul writes, "For now we see in a mirror, dimly, but then we will see face to face. Now I know only

28

in part; then I will know fully, even as I am fully known."[1] Believers have typically—and incorrectly, I believe—interpreted this passage as a kind of claim about when evidence will be so overwhelming that faith passes into knowledge. Instead, I would argue that the *dim mirror* offers a kind of clarity that a clear mirror cannot. What is seen in the light of stained glass is not visible in the light of clear glass. This is the stained-glass flip I think religious life requires. For believers, religious beliefs are clear, straightforward claims that theoretically could be confirmed or falsified by evidence. What the believer is asked to have faith in is not the living of a certain kind of life, but a belief that their religious claims will be confirmed once all the evidence is in. Of course, they also claim that all the evidence will not be in until the end of time.

The addiction that believers have to evidence is shared by unbelievers. Both sides believe that faith requires evidence. The believer thinks there is sufficient evidence without realizing that if there were, faith would be destroyed. The unbeliever thinks there is insufficient evidence without realizing that within the parameters of the Third Catch, lack of evidence is one of the conditions that makes faith possible. The two sides are locked in a contest where the loser is the winner and neither side wants to lose. Using the Third Catch as a reminder, the liberated religious realize that evidence plays no role in religious living, which means that the religious life is not about belief or faith. If evidence did play a role, the transcendent choice of religious living would be diminished to a choice between the reasonable and the unreasonable.

This leads us to another belief mattress that prevents believers from having to confront absolute grief. It is the mattress of belief in supernatural interventions into human life. This is the typical definition of miracles. The liberated religious do not look for supernatural interventions. It needs to be noted that even in the belief paradigm, miracles have been problematic. In the New Testament, it is unclear whether miracles were meant to foster belief in the divinity of Jesus or were impediments that distracted people from the call Jesus was actually trying to give. If the former, the miracles would provide evidence that would eliminate the possibility of belief for those who witnessed them. Subsequent generations would have to believe in the testimony of those witnesses. If the latter, then the New Testament was already trying to fight against the belief paradigm by stating that evidence is antithetical to faith. Both attitudes are reflected in John 6 where on

---

1. 1 Cor 13:12 NRSV.

one hand, Jesus feeds the multitude with a few pieces of bread and fish and on the other hand, Jesus says that what really matters is seeing the *miracle beyond the miracle* and recognizing that he is the bread of life. In fact, he says that some people cannot see the truth because they are hung up on the miracle.[2]

I would like to make a few observations about the miracles of Jesus as they are reported in the gospels. While accepting these observations is not necessary for liberated religious living, they may help free some believers from the belief paradigm and help some unbelievers reenter significant discussions about religious life. First, as I have already mentioned, miracles seem to be presented as providing evidence that Jesus was divine. Wherever evidence is regarded as important, belief and doubt are always options. Despite Jesus's miracles, many people, including the disciples themselves, are reported as having doubts even after witnessing the miracles. Among many scriptures that could be cited, the disciples' inability to imagine how they would feed the multitude in Mark 8:1–10 makes no sense if they had already witnessed Jesus performing the feeding miracle in Mark 6:30–44. If the supposed miracles leave room for doubt, then they must not have been the events that the gospels describe. This would suggest that something other than the miracle itself was needed in order for the miracle to be counted as evidence for the divinity of Jesus. If something else is required, however, the miracles are not really about evidence.

If Jesus actually did the miracles he is reported to have done, one would assume that those miracles would have provided pretty convincing evidence, yet many were not convinced. It is odd that believers today are more impressed by Jesus's miracles than the disciples who supposedly witnessed them. The significant difference between modern believers and first-century believers is that modern believers take the scientific or clear-glass paradigm for granted and apply it when interpreting miracle stories. While the correspondence theory of truth has always been present, it was not elevated to paradigmatic status until the Enlightenment. I do not think that first-century people regarded miracles as providing the kind of evidence that the clear-glass belief paradigm demands of propositional claims. The miracles were not performed to convince skeptics. What makes us different from New Testament people is that if something miraculous

---

2. John 6:1–14 for the feeding of the multitude; 6:25–35 for Jesus's suggestion that the people are letting their love of miraculous bread interfere with their ability to see the bread of life.

occurred today we would immediately conduct a scientific investigation and pronounce it unexplained or explained. Those who take the acts to be unexplained miracles would choose the mysterious and believing path. Those who think miracles can always be explained choose the explanatory and unbelieving path. The liberated religious, on the other hand, grant the unbelievers reasonable rejection of the miraculous because that rejection is the path toward *zero living* that makes seeing the miracle beyond the miracle possible.

D. Z. Phillips relays a story from Peter Winch about a statue of the Virgin Mary that purportedly wept. Believers accepted that the statue's weeping was a miracle of the type I have been discussing. Unbelievers argued that there must be a nonreligious alternative explanation for the phenomenon. In what I would call a response that borders on a liberated religious response, one woman said, "Why shouldn't the Holy Mother weep over the sins of the world?"[3] I say that her response borders on a liberated religious response because it does not go all the way and explicitly state that the miraculous claims made by believers prevent both them and unbelievers from interpreting the statue's tears in a transcendent way. A liberated religious person would reject the supernatural or mysterious explanation because that would provide evidence that both supports and defeats the possibility of belief. At the same time, the liberated religious person would reject the unbelievers's rejection because that would also be playing the evidentiary game of the clear-glass or belief paradigm. The liberated religious person, having made these two rejections very clear, would then say the kind of thing that the woman said in Winch's account. By rejecting both the believer's supernatural explanation and the unbeliever's naturalistic explanation, the liberated religious person is seeing the statue in a different light. Appreciating and affirming the woman's comment about the statue crying for the sins of the world is to interpret the event in the light of stained-glass windows. This light fills us with wonder and helps us see ourselves differently than the clear windows of the belief paradigm. It is to see the miracle beyond the miracle.

Because we are in the belief paradigm, it is believers and unbelievers who frame the debate about the evidence for or against faith. *ZeroTheology* resists this framing by not practicing lazy tolerance. If you are incapable of living as if miracles do not occur, the worst-case scenario, then the transcendent religious life is not possible for you. If you are unwilling to

3. Phillips, *Problem of Evil*, 17.

accept that miracles may be religious expressions of something other than propositional claims, the transcendent life is not possible for you either. This is not the same type of judgment that occurs when believers condemn or seek to punish those with whom they disagree. This is simply the kind of intolerance that says, "if you are unwilling to learn this particular game, you will be unable to play." If you really want to be liberated from the belief paradigm you have to stop being a believer or an unbeliever.

Related to the fact that some eyewitnesses were prepared to have doubts about Jesus is the fact that miracle workers were not rare in the ancient world. One is even referenced in Luke 9:49–50.[4] I would suggest that this is probably the case in any culture that does not inhabit the clear-glass paradigm of correspondence. It is not that supernatural miracles once occurred and then stopped occurring once science ascended. It is that things once regarded as miraculous ceased to be so regarded. Even today's fundamentalists do not live in the stained-glass paradigm of the ancient world. In fact, fundamentalism disrespects the scriptures it supposedly reveres by not acknowledging that they were composed in a different world under a different sort of metaphorical light.

The fact that Jesus was not the only wonder-worker in the first century should dramatically alter our perception of miracles. If different people can perform wondrous acts, then the performance of such an act would not necessarily set one of them apart as divine. But if the work is not enough to set the wonder-worker apart as divine, then the reported point of Jesus performing miracles in order to convince people is absurd. Why would Jesus perform miracles in order to convince people he was divine if he inhabited a world where miracles were not evidence of divinity? When the gospels claim that Jesus performed miracles as evidence to convince people he was divine and then express consternation that people are not convinced, their consternation is not the same as modern scientists who are frustrated with people who do not accept the evidence for evolution. Evidence in the clear-glass belief paradigm is not the same as evidence in the stained-glass religious paradigm. The fact that both utilize "evidence" hides the fact that they are using the word in very different ways.

It may be that there was always a nonreligious alternative explanation for Jesus's miracles. I regard that as a requirement if people are to be free

---

4. "John answered, 'Master, we saw someone casting out demons in your name, and we tried to stop him, because he does not follow with us.' But Jesus said to him, 'Do not stop him; for whoever is not against you is for you'" (Luke 9:49–50 NRSV).

to enter into religious living. But the miracles of Jesus are not presented as if they are just one possible explanation among many. This is because a miraculous claim is a religious claim on steroids. The traditional interpretation seems to be that in order to be a miracle, the miraculous event must overwhelm all other alternative explanations. This is because they are supposed to reveal the power of God or Jesus. If miracles are not earth-shattering and mind-blowing, then they are not really miracles at all. If miracles are not convincing, they are not miraculous. If they are convincing, they destroy the possibility of faith. I see no religious role for the typical understanding of miracles to play.

The better way of interpreting miracle stories from scripture is to see them as literary creations that serve as parables of performance. While his miracles were not always earth-shattering and mind-blowing, Jesus's parables often were. The parables were not told to convince people that Jesus was divine. In fact, we are told in Mark 4 that the purpose of teaching in parables is not to convince but to determine who has ears to hear and who does not, which may be another way of saying, to distinguish the liberated religious from those trapped in the belief paradigm.[5] Given that the gospels were written forty to seventy years after the time of Jesus, and given the fact that wonder-workers were not unheard of in the ancient world, it seems more likely that miracle stories are literary creations meant to have dramatic performative effect. The writers of the gospels inhabited a world where miracles were accepted, so I do not think they used the stories in manipulative or inauthentic ways. I think they simply used the miracles to paint their differing portraits because along with Hebrew Scriptures and oral traditions, miracles were a part of their first-century palette. The miracles provided a way to put flesh and blood on the more didactic act of telling parables. They are dramatic presentations of problems facing the Christians in the communities to which a particular gospel is addressed.

It may be that Jesus's calming the storm in Mark 4:35–41 has more to do with Christianity's difficulty moving from a primary Jewish clientele to a predominantly Gentile clientele than with actually stopping a storm at sea. The storm occurs as Jesus and the disciples move from Jewish to Gentile territory.[6] The healing of the Gerasene demoniac in Mark 5:1–20 may be a dramatic portrayal of the freedom the gospel promises to those who are

5. Mark 4:1–20.
6. Juel, *Mark*, 78.

in the chains of Roman oppression.[7] The raising of Jairus's twelve-year-old daughter and the healing of the woman who had bled for twelve years in Mark 5:21–43 may be about the liberation the gospel offers to women who were made ritualistically unclean and cut off from the community rather than about a man with superpowers.[8] I am willing to concede that we may not know enough about the first-century world to know how to interpret every miracle reported in the gospels. Nor am I prepared to claim that every miracle is a political performance. I imagine that others play other kinds of roles within the narratives. However, I do believe these kinds of explanations are better than the easily refuted idea that Jesus performed unconvincing miracles in order to convince people that he was divine.

As important as it may be to understand the miraculous events portrayed in the Gospels, it is not as important as understanding why human beings have a need to believe such things are possible. It is clear that believing in most miracles comes from a need that is a reaction to circumstantial limitations. These limitations usually involve the kind of physical, emotional, and political limitations that comprise circumstantial grief. We run up against something that we cannot do, and we would like to imagine that we can overcome the limitation. We cannot feed people with the food on hand, so we want a miracle to make the impossible possible. A loved one has a terminal illness, and we want a miracle to take the illness away. Supernatural interventions in real life, as opposed to the ones described in scripture, are always short on evidence. They tend to thrive where explanations are fuzzy. We do not typically see tumors inside a body so we pray for miracles to reduce them. We do see broken or amputated limbs, and people do not typically pray for them to mend or regrow before their eyes. If people did pray and limbs regrew as a result, YouTube videos would abound.

Miracles also serve to make us feel important. If I can name a miracle that has occurred in my life, I can feel as though God is paying attention to me and my needs. I am convinced that occasionally, though not always, people report a miraculous event in order to promote themselves or their own interests. I once heard a candidate for a student government position at a seminary tell an assembled group that Jesus had appeared to her the previous night and told her that he wanted her to get elected. I almost got up and said that Jesus had appeared to me the previous week and told me that he was going to play a practical joke on that candidate. When people

---

7. Juel, *Mark*, 80.

8. Juel, *Mark*, 82–89.

make miraculous claims that are self-promoting, they turn what could be a liberated religious expression of wonder into a manipulative tool that the belief paradigm makes readily available.

I have indicated that the circumstantial/absolute distinction plays an important role in *ZeroTheology*. I make a distinction between circumstantial miracles and absolute miracles. Circumstantial miracles are miracles that relieve the limiting circumstances in life. Food that feeds the hungry would be the product of a circumstantial miracle. The same would be true of healing- and escape-based miracles. The miracles of Jesus, as well as the miracles performed by God in the Hebrew Scriptures, typically fall into the circumstantial miracle category. While these miracles address the circumstantial griefs of life, they do not touch absolute grief. The only miracles in the Christian tradition that I can imagine putting in the absolute miracle category are the Virgin Birth and the Resurrection of Jesus. I will consider these miracles in later sections.

When a person chooses the religious life without needing to believe in miracles, that person has a life that transcends the evidentiary problems that come with the belief paradigm. This avoids the evidence idolatry that Jesus confronts in John 6 about the people who follow because of the miraculous feeding and the point he makes again about Thomas in John 20. By not needing miracles, the liberated religious resolve to live courageously in a world where some limitations are final and accepted. Everyone dies, regardless of miracles or prayer. The righteous often suffer because of their righteousness. The wicked often prosper because of their wickedness. Cancer comes to the just and the unjust. Religious living is not something that is done to try to control these limitations and realities. Religious living is a compassionate and courageous response that is only possible within these limitations and realities. To try to get rid of the limitations and realities is to try to get rid of the possibility of religious living. Believers spend all of their time trying to remove the conditions that make religious life possible in the first place. The thing that we need to get rid of in order to live a liberated religious life is the miracle mattress that tries to keep us from facing the possibility of absolute grief. The point is not that miracles do not or could not occur. The point is that those who are liberated from the belief paradigm do not need them and see evidence for them as an impediment to transcendent living.

The only God that satisfies
is the God that does not satisfy.

If you are completely satisfied with God, you are a believer. If you are completely unsatisfied with God, you are an unbeliever. If you are completely satisfied with being completely unsatisfied with God, you are the liberated religious. Those who do not seek the satisfaction of belief in a present God are unlikely to choose the religious life, although they are the only ones who can.

The only concept of God that meets the conditions of religious living in *Zero Theology* is a concept that is satisfied with dissatisfaction. This is to restate the previous Catch-22s in a different way. The First Catch teaches that one will never be satisfied if one thinks a religious journey leads to a destination. The Second Catch insists that faith must not be so necessary that one cannot live without it. The Third Catch states that any evidence that would confirm God's existence would destroy the possibility of faith. The Fourth Catch says that to be completely satisfied with one's concept of God is to commit idolatry. To insist that God is present and vocal in ways that leave no room for dissatisfaction is the idolatry of the belief paradigm.

This coincides with the idea that for any straightforward religious claim there must be an alternative, credible, straightforward, nonreligious claim if people are to be free. Of course, scripture and tradition are replete with revelation stories that supposedly demonstrate God's presence in completely satisfying ways that would seem to eradicate the possibility of an unsatisfactory absence. As I stated in my comments on miracles, I am not convinced that this is the way these stories should be interpreted. However,

I cannot help thinking that the traditional interpretation prevails because human beings are notoriously unhappy with dissatisfaction, especially when they are trying to convince others to adopt their religious views. This craving for satisfaction is the basic mistake made by believers. It is also the traditional definition of and the continual motivation for idolatry, whether the idol is built with hands or with the mind. Idolatry is the hallmark of belief. Both the liberated religious and unbelievers reject this idolatry. This rejection of idolatry is why the liberated religious path makes no sense to believers who do not recognize their beliefs as idols. Because unbelievers equate religion with belief in idols, they have a difficult time understanding the non-idolatrous path of the liberated religious.

God is unsatisfying. Believers will disagree and assert that they are completely satisfied with God. This is their idolatry. When I say that God is unsatisfying, I am not saying that God is nonexistent because that is the kind of statement made by an unbeliever from within the belief paradigm. Nor am I saying that no one ever experiences any religious satisfaction in life. I am saying that it is dissatisfaction with God that provides the context for the occasional satisfying experience. Another way of speaking about satisfaction and dissatisfaction is to speak of God's presence and absence. The context that gives God's presence its power in life is a context defined by God's absence. If God has an essential attribute, it is absence.

The difference between religious claims and factual claims brings God's absence into focus. The very idea of divine revelation, so important in the history of Christian thought, is a response to God's absence. If God were present no one could claim to speak for God and no one could claim a unique channel of communication with the divine. The very notion of inspired scripture or orthodox belief is based on the assumption that God is not present to speak for Godself. Prayer, as it is popularly conceived, is also predicated on the idea that God is absent. If God were present, prayer would not be our form of communication. The notion that God is present and that prayer is a form of communication with an invisible deity is another mattress that needs to be surrendered because it operates in the belief paradigm and demands conceptual satisfaction even though prayer requests often go unfulfilled.

If God is absent, God is also silent. When you scream into the whirlwind like Job, you get silence. After all, that is the effect of what God said to Job in chapter 38. What God said to Job could also have been communicated with silence but that would have hindered the desired dramatic effect of the scene. Like the miracles of Jesus, this is about dramatic effect, not historical reporting. When Jesus calls from the cross, he is met with silence. How else would we expect God to respond? If God responded with presence and voice, as believers expect God to do at the Last Judgment, then everything we think about God and religious living would disappear. The idea that God will come into history at some point in the future and speak judgments on human beings only makes sense if God is not doing those things in the present. If God is here now, then there is no need for God to come in the future.

I realize that metaphoricists or progressive Christians will respond that they do not believe that God is literally coming at a future time to make judgments. They will say that they believe God is always and already present. Again, this is a religious claim that can only be freely affirmed if there is evidence to the contrary. If God were present we would not need progressive Christians to proclaim it. There are scriptural and traditional examples of God's presence being presented as absence. In addition to Job and Jesus, there is Elijah's experience in 1 Kings 19:12 and the psalmist's anguish in Psalm 13. Christian mysticism, when it does not fall into a confused religious version of skepticism, also expresses God's absence through the idea of dissatisfaction. It is the absence of God that makes the religious life about the journey rather than the destination. If the destination were ever reached and God made present, we would lose the capacity for religious living. The religious journey is not a search for an absent God; it is the absent God that motivates the religious journey and makes it powerful.

Belief in divine revelation is another mattress that must go if we are to escape the belief paradigm and confront the possibility of absolute grief with courage and compassion. The whole idea of divine revelation (and its cousin, divine inspiration) is to somehow grant human authority divine credibility. This is an attempt to make God present and vocal while taking advantage of God's absence and silence. The idea that the Bible is God's presence and voice is the most obvious example of this. Scripture does not claim this for itself and could not even if it so desired. Since scripture is composed of different books written at different times by different authors who had no idea that their writing would be part of a compilation, no single author can make a claim for the whole—just as no single book in a particular library can speak on behalf of all the other books in that particular library. Second Timothy 3:16 cannot speak for the library that the church has chosen to call "holy scripture."[1] Scriptural authority is a claim made by the church. The church relies on the ideas of revelation and inspiration to undergird the claim that the Bible is authoritative, but it is the church's own authority that is being asserted.

The religious concept of revelation is the counterpart to the philosophical concept of epistemological foundations. Just as some philosophers attempt to get at the "really real" upon which all scientific claims rest, religious people use revelation to justify the other claims they wish to make about the world. In philosophy, the further one gets down to the supposed foundations of knowledge the more authority the philosopher wants to claim. In religion, the higher one climbs on the ladder of revelation the more authority the religious leader can claim. Revelations are like skyhooks, and the belief is that these skyhooks are closer to God and lend credibility to those who can access them. This desire for foundations is generated by the assumptions of the belief paradigm.

The need that belief in divine revelation satisfies is the need to have a present and vocal deity in order to grant some sense of certainty in life. The fear is that, without revelation, a chaotic relativism will ascend. Setting aside the fact that human community and the possibility of communication make this kind of radical relativism impossible, it is the uncertain conditions that prevail in life that make religious living possible in the first place. This is not a new notion. In some ways, *Zero Theology* is a Christian restatement of stoicism or of the sentiments expressed in Rudyard Kipling's poem "If." What we surrender when we give up the need for the mattress of revelation is the need to gain credibility or authority for ourselves and the need to have an external authority control the ways human beings live. This is not to say that human beings control everything in life or that there are no limitations to what humans can accomplish. It is to give up the idea that we can explain why certain things happen based on moral or religious grounds. This is the actual point of Job.

In attempting to break out of the belief paradigm, I have suggested that we move away from belief or disbelief and toward the imaginative *as if* described in Constantin Stanislavsky's approach to acting. In my opinion, the metaphorical exemplar of the belief paradigm is the *five blind men and the elephant* metaphor. This well-worn parable suggests that truth, reality,

---

1. "All scripture is inspired by God and is useful for teaching, for reproof, for correction, and for training in righteousness, so that everyone who belongs to God may be proficient, equipped for every good work" (2 Tim 3:16–17 NRSV).

the world, or God is like an elephant and that religions, individuals, and cultures are like blind men. The parable suggests that the blind man who feels the trunk thinks that the whole truth is like the trunk. The blind man who feels the ear thinks that truth or reality is like the ear. The point seems to be that each perspective is inadequate and that when we listen to or honor other perspectives, we come to appreciate more of the truth or more about the reality of God. While I applaud the honoring of diverse perspectives, I find fault with the presumption that there is a single independent religious truth that is the shared target of these diverse perspectives.

The *five blind men and the elephant* model is an example that works when we presume the correspondence theory of truth. Even though total knowledge of the elephant is inaccessible, the presumption is that the elephant is there. As I have already indicated, this model claims that a sentence, thought, or belief is true only if it matches up with the external reality to which it supposedly refers. This is the model that drives the way scientists understand the scientific process. For this reason, much philosophy of science has been focused on verification and falsification. As these terms imply, the key concern is determining whether a scientific claim is verified or falsified when that claim is measured against a corresponding piece of the objective world. Though Thomas Kuhn's *Structure of Scientific Revolutions* suggests that there is more to science than this one-to-one correspondence between claim and fact, it is generally the case that scientists go about their daily tasks using the tools and concepts that work on correspondence presumptions.

In *ZeroTheology*, I wish to get rid of the elephant in the room, which, in the belief paradigm, is the elephant in the room. It is what keeps people trapped. It is what drives believers to make claims about God and the world that create conflict with unbelievers. It is also why they resist the idea that for every straightforward religious claim there must be a credible nonreligious claim. I am not saying that words never refer or that there are no uses for the *blind men and the elephant* metaphor; I am simply saying that there is no reason, other than tradition, to presume that religion must share a paradigm with science. Stained glass should not be measured by the criteria used to judge the adequacy of transparent glass. It is idolatry that keeps both believers and unbelievers insisting that it should. Here I wish to shift us from thinking about the elephant in the room to thinking about the *beetle in the box*.

Ludwig Wittgenstein used the beetle in the box thought experiment in what is regarded as his argument against the possibility of private language. He used the thought experiment to talk about how *pain* gains its meaning. I will be applying the thought experiment to God rather than pain because although they are different kinds of concepts, they share the important feature of not gaining their meaning from correspondence. The beetle in the box thought experiment is found in paragraph 293 of *Philosophical Investigations*. Imagine that everyone had a box. You can only see inside your box and no one else can see inside anyone else's box. It is possible that we could all use the word *beetle* when talking about the contents of our boxes and this would be true even if none of us had the same thing in our boxes, if the things in our boxes constantly changed, or even if there was nothing in our boxes. The use of the word *beetle* is not determined by your private experience of whatever is in your box. The word gains its meaning from the way the community uses the word.[2] Because the contents of the box may differ, change, or not exist at all, the term *beetle* in the game does not refer to the contents of the box, whatever they may be, unless you are, as Wittgenstein says elsewhere, "playing with words."[3]

In paragraph 293, Wittgenstein is specifically talking about how the word *pain* gains its meaning. When expressing pain, we are expressing a private sensation that is unavailable to others and beyond doubt to ourselves. To feel a pain is to have pain. One cannot make a mistake about feeling pain. Wittgenstein employs the beetle in the box thought experiment to show that even though people have private sensations that are unavailable to others, the pain expressions we share with others do not gain their meaning by referring to those private sensations. They gain their meaning from public agreement and usage. If you do not talk or act like someone who is in pain, I will not believe that you are in pain. Even if you exhibit all the agreed-upon pain behaviors, I can still doubt your pain in a way that I cannot doubt my own pain; but more importantly, my doubting of your pain is something you can understand, even if you are angry with me for doubting it.

Our private sensations of pain are different from our personal experiences of God in important ways. Unlike pain, God is not a sensation that cannot be doubted. God is not an itch. To think you are in pain is no different from your being in pain. To think you are experiencing God is different

2. Wittgenstein, *Philosophical Investigations*, 100.

3. Wittgenstein, *Philosophical Investigations*, 32.

because it is possible for you to be mistaken. What you perceive as God can be explained in other ways—as "an undigested bit of beef," perhaps.[4] In fact, this possibility of alternative explanations of personal experiences of God reflects the requirement that for any religious claim, there must be an alternative nonreligious claim if religious belief is to be entered into freely. That you are possibly mistaken is proven by the fact that people, even those within your religious community, are more predisposed to doubt your religious testimony of a personal experience with God then they are to doubt your expression of being in pain. Sincerity is a concern for believers precisely because they are unable to corroborate the testimony of your personal experience and they are less sure that you are describing something that is consistent with their conception of God. These concerns are not usually present with pain. What pain and God have in common is that neither is able to point to what it purportedly refers to in a publicly verifiable way and this inability to refer means that both pain expressions and God conceptions rely on the agreement of a community. Pain expressions are not unintelligible because they lack a verifiable referent and neither are religious expressions. We make a mistake in religion when we think that correspondence is necessary for religious expressions to have meaning, but that is because the belief paradigm compels us to convert religious expressions into propositions about God. As we will see in a future section, a similar mistake is made when we believe that pain expressions must always be conveyors of information about pain.

Private religious experiences are derived from the social priority of concept formation and form of life. They are subject to criticism within faith communities if the testifier reports something contrary to what the community believes or if the testifier does not behave in ways that the community accepts. The importance of the beetle in the box thought experiment in ZeroTheology is that it shows that human communities are perfectly capable of using words in meaningful ways even though those words do not refer to a shared target in the "objective" world. I use the beetle in the box thought experiment to make the minimal claim that the word God, like the word beetle, need not correspond with anything to be meaningful. God need not be like the partially perceived elephant. God can be like the beetle, which may or may not be in the box.

One may wonder what difference it makes whether we see religion as talking about a divine elephant or a divine beetle. One may wonder if this

4. Dickens, Christmas Carol, 26.

difference between the elephant and the beetle differs from the debate over William James's squirrel. In his famous lecture "What Pragmatism Means," William James describes an argument he encountered between a group of people walking in the woods. A squirrel is on one side of a tree. A person approaches from the other side. As the person walks around the tree, the squirrel moves in corresponding fashion so that the tree is always between the squirrel and the person. When the person has completely circumnavigated the tree, without ever seeing the squirrel, has the person walked round the squirrel or not?[5] James suggests that there is no right answer to this argument because it all comes down to what is meant by walking around the squirrel. If one means passing to the north, east, south, west and back to north, then the person walked around the squirrel. If one means passing from the front of the squirrel to its left, back, right and front again, then the person did not walk around the squirrel. For James and pragmatists, such debates are illusory because they have no practical consequences in real life. In light of James's squirrel discussion, we can ascertain whether or not a religious elephant or religious beetle makes a difference.

There is certainly some similarity in that whether we see religious truth as a divine elephant or divine beetle is based on how we choose to frame the conversation. Believers and unbelievers often converse with each other as though they occupy the same frame. This is why they often fail to notice that they use words like *evidence* in very different ways. They frame religious truth as being about a divine elephant so the issue is whether or not religious claims measure up to the same level of scrutiny with which scientific claims are measured. Believers think that their religious claims do measure up. Unbelievers do not think that these religious claims measure up. Both agree that the elephant in the room is named *truth*, but when God is added to that truth, believers see a divine rider and unbelievers see none. Nevertheless, they believe they are arguing about the same elephant.

The reason the debate makes a difference is that if we can shift from seeing religious expressions as either adequate literal or inadequate metaphorical descriptions of some external divine reality (elephant) and recognize them as dependent upon the conceptual agreement of a community (beetle) then we can break free from the belief paradigm that tells us that being religious, like being scientific, is about aligning one's beliefs with an external reality. When believers and unbelievers converse, they are not

---

5. James, "What Pragmatism Means," in *Pragmatism and The Meaning of Truth*, 27–28.

typically aware of the fact that they actually do not share the same frame and are talking past each other. This does not mean that they occupy different paradigms, only that they operate out of different frames within the belief paradigm. This difference remains hidden because both think they are having the same conversation about the same elephant in the room or the same squirrel in the tree. What James's squirrel offers us is the notion that framing what counts as criteria is done within communities in specifically contextual ways. The elephant model promotes the idea that all contexts have access to the same elephant. James's squirrel brings specific contexts into play while assuming the same squirrel. Wittgenstein's beetle goes one step further and says that when it comes to certain kinds of expressions, what a beetle is or is not rests solely within the context of a community. By placing God's absence at the center of its conception of God, *ZeroTheology* avoids the existence/nonexistence arguments of the belief paradigm in favor of choosing to live a certain kind of transcendent life. The liberated religious do not need to believe that God is like the elephant or the squirrel. This lack of need makes God like the beetle.

In the belief paradigm, one's religious beliefs are evaluated on two criteria. The first criterion is whether the belief is true or not. Does the religious belief correspond with the way things really are? This approach works in science because there are agreed-upon criteria and agreed-upon processes that allow competitive parties to determine winners and losers. In religion, there is no agreement between differing religious communities and only tenuous agreement within a religious community. Science has some idea of the elephant in the room and has tools to measure aspects of it. These measurements are available to anyone who learns how to use the tools.

Religion has no elephant, and if it did, it would violate the conditions of the Third Catch where evidence would destroy the possibility of living religiously. In religion, it has always been about beetles in boxes or gods in hearts where the only judge of whether or not someone is being religious in the "right" way is determined by the community that makes up the rules. The problem is that religious communities pretend that the rules were made up by an independent but inaccessible God and communicated through divine revelation. Religion wants to have its elephant and its beetle too. The divine elephant communicates to a religious community but since the religious community has no access to the divine elephant that can be publicly verified, the religious community governs itself in the same way a community would govern itself regarding the use of "beetle."

I have already touched on the second criterion utilized by the belief paradigm to evaluate beliefs. This criterion is sincerity. In believer faith communities, it is usually not enough to have correct belief. Because they are aware that there is no non-community-based publicly verifiable way of determining whether one's belief is correct or not, they shift judgment to whether one's belief is sincere or not. In science, the sincerity of the scientist making a claim is irrelevant to the claim itself. Potentially, a scientist could make a claim or discovery about which she has serious misgivings. Such a thought is alien to religious claims. Doubt plays a different and more significant role in the religious person's faith than it does in the scientist's faith in a theory. The belief paradigm, however, directs both the believer and the unbeliever to privilege the value of sincerity. For the believer, anything less than sincerity is an indictment of one's faith. Unbelievers agree, which is why they have such sincere arguments with believers. This is why both groups are suspicious of any talk of escaping the belief paradigm.

By being self-consciously aware that its use of religious concepts is formed by the community (like beetles in boxes), the community can be free from the pitfalls and divisions of the belief paradigm. This is not to say that the religious community should see God as a social construction; that would be too satisfying to nonbelievers and too dissatisfying to believers. It is to say that where God's absence is appreciated as essential to God's character, there is no need to posit a present but invisible deity. Nothing is gained by making the assertion that God must be "really real" in the same way that planets and stars are in the scientific vocabulary. To do so would be to commit the idolatry of presence, which is another way of saying the idolatry of the correspondence theory of truth. To make that claim is to be completely satisfied with God and does nothing but play the part of a mattress that prevents the claimant from confronting the possibility of absolute grief.

One casualty of surrendering the "really real" is the value of sincerity. But this is only because when the belief paradigm is escaped, sincerity is no longer regarded as the highest virtue. One could say that this is the point of the New Testament book of James, which defines faithfulness as a way of life rather than belief. This may be because while it is possible to be *double-minded* in the belief paradigm that privileges the *tongue* of propositional phrases, it is not possible to be *double-actioned* when it comes to living a certain kind of life.[6]

The problem with giving up the divine elephant is that for both the believer and the unbeliever, such a move seems like surrendering to atheism. If God is not "out there" or "really real," then what is the point of the religious life? The liberated religious, on the other hand, consider such a move not to be a surrender at all but to be a requirement for religious or transcendent living. The refusal of believers to surrender their divine elephant is similar to the refusal of Job's friends to surrender the moral and reasonable God they worshipped. Such an idol was a mattress that prevented them from having to confront the possibility that God is not a moral agent who plays by the rules of human reasonability.

I have said that religious life is a response and that one of the things that it responds to is the existential angst of absolute grief. Religious life also responds to beauty, love, and companionship. As long as we regard religious life as being about belief, rather than an *as if* response to absolute grief, the belief paradigm will force us to see God as an explanation. Seeking to be completely satisfied we speak of God as the Creator in an attempt to make God present and vocal. Theology has traditionally tried to explain the relationship between a present God and a fallen creation. In my opinion, theology should get out of the explanation business and devote itself to a kind of poetry. This kind of poetry may not be very poetic, but by employing parables, paradoxes and Catch-22s, *ZeroTheology*, like poetry, opens up new ways of conceiving human life without making theological explanations about facts in the world. This is to say that theology should articulate the wonder and enlightenment that comes from seeing ourselves in the light of stained-glass windows rather than trying to explain or justify the God that the clear-glass paradigm demands.

The belief paradigm traps believers in a conceptual loop that keeps them pursuing two contradictory goals. In his classic paper "How to Make Our Ideas Clear," Charles Sanders Peirce describes a persistent problem that often sabotages attempts to gain clarity:

> One singular deception of this sort, which often occurs, is to mistake the sensation produced by our own unclearness of thought for a character of the object we are thinking. Instead of perceiving that the obscurity is purely subjective, we fancy that we contemplate a quality of the object which is essentially mysterious; and if

6. See Jas 4:8; 3:8; and 2:15–17.

our conception be afterward presented to us in a clear form we do not recognize it as the same, owing to the absence of the feeling of unintelligibility.[7]

Peirce has put his finger on an addiction that the belief paradigm promotes. This addiction creates division between believers and unbelievers because it compels believers to make claims that strike unbelievers as unreasonable. This addiction also baptizes conceptual confusion in the name of divine mystery.

As I have stated, in order for belief to not be compulsory in the belief paradigm, any straightforward religious claim should be accompanied by a credible nonreligious alternative claim. If there are no nonreligious explanations available it is either because the religious expression is not making the kind of straightforward claim that could be verified or falsified (like a Catch-22) or because the religious claim is being made in an area not currently occupied by some other field of expertise. This second type of claim is sometimes referred to as a "god of the gaps" kind of claim. This is another way that believers try to make God present and vocal. It is an attempt to justify their religious beliefs. This makes it a mattress they use to avoid the possibility of confronting the worst-case scenario of absolute grief. An example might be that since physicists are currently unable to reconcile general relativity with quantum mechanics, and since quantum mechanics seems to defy well-tested experiences in the non-quantum world, this inability to explain must reveal something about the mysteries of a divine mind. In other words, this "gap" invites theologians to offer divine or spiritual explanations. Theological explanation is theology at its worst.

The obvious problem with the god of the gaps is that it is always refutable by the next breakthrough in human understanding. The "god" of the gaps has been evicted as gap after gap has been closed by increased understanding. The subtler problem with this type of theological explanation is that it is driven by the belief paradigm that compels theologians and philosophers of religion to offer explanations that gain their meaning from the evidential or scientific paradigm, even as these explanations are sometimes anti-scientific in content.

These flaws notwithstanding, believers keep moving the finish line because there is always some next mystery that needs to be explained. Like a version of Zeno's Paradox, believers use the possibility of endless division

7. Peirce, "How to Make Our Ideas Clear," in Houser and Kloesel, *Essential Peirce*, 1:130.

in the same way that creationists use it to insist that there is always a missing link in the evolutionary chain. While this flaw is fatal to god of the gaps explanations, it does not prevent believers from continuing to offer them. They do so because while they have a need for theological explanations they also have a need for unexplained mysteries. This is a trap because the religious believer expects there to be mysteries that can only be explained theologically and then expects those theological explanations to include mystery. Peirce is getting at this fallacy in his statement about confusing a lack of clarity in our thinking for a mysterious quality of what we are considering.

The believer has to be on the defensive whenever one of these mysteries is explained by nonreligious means. Because the believer associates religious belief with unexplained mysteries, the believer has to keep raising the bar on what counts as explanation so that the feeling that accompanied the previous but now explained mystery can be preserved. One of the believer's core desires, explanation, is at odds with another core desire, mystery. Since the belief paradigm requires that both be preserved, God is used as both the explainer and the preserver of the mysterious feeling. Believer theologians, who tend to think they are in the explanation business, oscillate between explanation and mystery so that when an objection is made against one they can retreat to the other. This keeps believers insulated from other kinds of explanations. This defense of mystery is actually a defense of ignorance. Because it is defensive, it is self-serving and totally understandable. It is not, however, the transcendent living of the religious life.

You can only feel safe when you are in danger.

You can only feel absolutely safe when you feel justifiably afraid. If you feel justifiably afraid, you will not feel circumstantially safe. When you are justifiably afraid, you are the most prepared to feel absolutely safe. Religious or transcendent safety is about feeling absolutely safe. Feeling absolutely safe is a religious attitude or a transcendent choice. It is perfectly reasonable to feel unsafe in situations where you are justifiably afraid. Ludwig Wittgenstein made very similar comments in his *Lecture on Ethics*.[1]

To appreciate the profundity of what is being claimed in this Catch-22, we need to commit what would otherwise be a Wittgensteinian sin. We need to commit ourselves to a standard definition of what the word *safe* usually means or how it is usually used. We do not do this out of an insistence on the standard dictionary usage. We do this because if we do not start with how *safe* is usually used we will not appreciate the creative way that religious people misuse it.

Safe is a circumstantial adjective describing one's condition or how one feels at a particular time and place. People are safe in their homes. Villages are safe behind walls. Nations feel safe if they have a strong military. Because it is a circumstantial adjective, it is easy to imagine conditions where people are not safe. They are not safe in a stormy sea. They are not safe if they lack shelter. Nations do not feel safe if they have a weak military and suspect their enemies are threatening. We learn to use the word *safe* in

1. Wittgenstein, *Lecture on Ethics*, 47.

49

particular circumstances, and within those circumstances it is easy to tell if someone is using the word correctly or not.

The Fifth Catch is describing the kind of misuse that Wittgenstein spoke about. As with grief, I am making a distinction between circumstantial and absolute approaches to a concept. As previously indicated, I borrow this, slightly amended, from Wittgenstein, who made a similar distinction between relative and absolute judgments of value.[2] To take a concept away from its circumstantial context and use it in an absolute way is to misuse the word. This misuse can lead to philosophical confusion. Words like *consciousness, truth, justice,* and *God* are primary examples of words that have led to mischief when philosophers and theologians have removed them from their circumstantial contexts. But that is because the misuse is unintentional and unnoticed. When we do the same with *safe* in a religious way, we are misusing the word on purpose, and this misuse opens up a transcendent choice not present to those who will not misuse it or to those who misuse it out of confusion.

To misuse *safe* or to speak of absolute safety is to describe a religious commitment that occurs in circumstances where one has no business feeling safe. If I can feel safe when I am in a storm at sea I can claim to feel safe even in the worst-case scenario. If I can feel safe when I lack shelter or when my defenses are weak and my enemies are threatening, then I have a safety that cannot be harmed by the circumstances of life. Absolute safety is what one feels when one feels safe even if one is attacked or harmed. As Wittgenstein puts it, feeling absolutely safe means feeling safe *no matter what happens,* even the worst-case scenario.[3] It is like confronting absolute grief and gaining absolute peace. Both *grief* and *peace* are being misused by *ZeroTheology* because they are words that describe feelings that transcend the circumstantial contexts that usually give them their meanings.

There are two different levels of absolute safety. The first level of absolute safety helps one feel safe regardless of the circumstantial dangers in which one finds oneself. This is the kind of absolute safety that has been described. When John Wesley sailed to America in 1736, he was impressed by the Moravians on the ship who were not afraid in the midst of a terrible storm. He was impressed by the absolute safety they felt while they were in circumstantial danger. Their safety, however, was founded on a mattress of belief that denied the possibility of absolute grief. The second level of

2. Wittgenstein, *Lecture on Ethics,* 44.

3. Wittgenstein, *Lecture on Ethics,* 47–48.

absolute safety is feeling safe in the presence of absolute danger. Would the Moravians have felt peaceful amidst the storm if they also lacked a belief that they would be taken care of in an afterlife? The person who feels absolutely safe in the face of absolute grief is the person who practices the kind of courage that the transcendent life requires.

Believers and unbelievers rebel at this misuse of concepts. Believers want a faith that makes them feel circumstantially safe forever. Unbelievers do not believe it makes sense to speak of any kind of safety other than circumstantial safety. The two sides argue over the same term and restrict its use to its circumstantial contexts. The liberated religious, on the other hand, knowingly commit a mistake though this is more of a poetic and new usage of a word than it is a mistake. To use a word differently from the way it has always been used is a creative act and a way of breaking free from the belief paradigm.

It is important to grasp and grant the usual usage of *safe* because that makes the misuse explicit. Another way of saying this is to say that the normal usage is perfectly reasonable. It is perfectly reasonable to feel safe when you are inside your home or behind strong walls. It is perfectly reasonable to feel vulnerable when you are exposed to the elements or on a treacherous road. It is also perfectly reasonable to carry a gun in order to make you feel safe from the circumstantial threats of the world.

To suggest a concrete example of how absolute safety would impact a current political debate, let us look at the issue of guns. Progressives completely miss the point when they argue from statistics about how owning a gun actually increases one's risk of being wounded or killed. It does not matter if that is statistically true; it feels unreasonable to people who never see themselves as a statistic but only imagine themselves in particular threatening circumstances where a gun might be useful. Whatever the case, arguments over guns inevitably break down to disputes over what is reasonable and unreasonable with both sides claiming to be on the side of reason.

By departing from the normal usage of *safe*, the liberated religious are able to mount a different sort of argument in the gun debate. They grant what progressives cannot. They grant that it is perfectly reasonable to own a gun. It is perfectly reasonable to desire some control over possible threats that may come your way. Every person has found himself or herself alone in a frightening situation. If we are honest, having a gun would make most of us feel safer when we find ourselves in threatening situations. What the liberated religious have to say in the dispute is not another accusation that those who want guns are unreasonable. In fact, it makes all the sense in the world. It is not, however, the transcendent choice of liberated religious living.

The transcendent choice says, "I will feel safe even without a gun." By making a distinction between absolute safety and circumstantial security, the religious choose a different path that is far more consistent with the Jesus who did not strike back at those who hit him and who asked his followers to turn the other cheek. The most honest way of responding to Jesus and his teachings would be to say that they are unreasonable at worst or non-reasonable at best. The most dishonest way of responding is to try to make Jesus's teachings reasonable. When one feels absolutely safe one does not seek circumstantial safety in something designed to inflict harm. This is a choice that transcends the reasonable/unreasonable debate. When one feels absolutely safe one is willing to prioritize courage and compassion over using any means necessary to maintain circumstantial safety.

To feel absolutely safe involves the giving up of the mattress named *security*. Again, this does not mean that vulnerable people should unreasonably expose themselves to greater vulnerability and potential victimization. Within a circumstantial context, it is perfectly reasonable and justifiable to take protective actions. People who are circumstantially safe are in no position to lecture those who are circumstantially vulnerable on what is reasonable or unreasonable when it comes to circumstantial security. It is enough to remind people that as reasonable as it may be, it is not the choice of transcendent living. This does not convey moral judgment. It is simply to convey that religious living is an absolute commitment that trumps circumstantial challenges.

One of the biggest threats to Christianity in the United States is that what was once seen as the circumstantial threat of violence has been elevated by some to the status of an absolute threat of violence. If the conditions of life are defined as absolutely threatening, it gives people who may be circumstantially justified in owning a gun a religious reason to have an absolute commitment to owning a gun. This is idolatry, and in this way the god worshipped by the gun believer is more of an abomination than the rejection of god by unbelievers. I am tempted to say that if gun believers see life as absolutely threatening, they have in practice given up on God and have accepted the worst-case scenario. They have accepted it, not with the courage and compassion of religious living but with the fear and self-righteousness of idolatrous living. If hope is the child of courage and acceptance, despair is the child of fear and anger. This obsession with safety is a mattress that must go if one is to live with the courage, compassion, and connection that come with liberated religious living in the face of absolute grief.

I would call what Wittgenstein defines as the feeling of absolute safety an attitude of absolute courage. This courage is what is required to confront and live with the pea of absolute grief. It takes real circumstantial courage to acquire some of the mattresses or needs that are necessary for human life and flourishing. It takes absolute courage, however, to realize that absolute grief will haunt human life *no matter what happens*, even the best-case scenario. It does not matter how many mattresses you put between you and grief. This awareness is what explains the disillusionment and boredom that often accompanies privileged living. It is behind clichés like "money can't buy happiness."

Just as there is a connection between circumstantial and absolute grief, there is a connection between circumstantial and absolute courage. I believe that people like Gandhi, Martin Luther King, and Jesus drew from the absolute courage each mustered to confront absolute grief and that this absolute courage served as a resource for the circumstantial courage that was required for each of them to confront the circumstantial griefs in life.

In Psalm 23 we encounter many of the characteristics of *Zero Theology's* approach to liberated religious living. Liberated religious living is not about want or need. Liberated religious living appreciates the circumstantial blessings in life and expresses gratitude for them. Liberated religious living feels absolutely safe while walking through the valley of the shadow. In fact, it is only in the valley of the shadow that absolute safety is even possible. The last affirming lines are examples of absolute gratitude and absolute safety. It is not about what happens after life is over; it is about living a certain kind of life "one's whole life long." This is a religious expression of safety. It is a religious expression because there is plenty of evidence to the contrary. God is absent, troubles mount, death wins. Into this reality, the psalmist proclaims a safety even though God is absent, troubles mount, and death wins. This is the transcendent choice of religious living. To say that the Lord is my shepherd is to say that I feel safe even if the worst-case scenario is true. It is not a proposition about the Lord's presence, for if the Lord were present, the psalm would be unnecessary.

SIXTH CATCH

Mystery is only possible
when explanation makes it unnecessary.

You can only feel absolute wonder at things that are explained. If something is unexplained, then what you feel is unintelligibility. When something is explained, you lose wonder. Absolute wonder can only be expressed by those who accept the explanations that normally eradicate wonder. Wonder is not connected to unintelligibility just as the liberated religious life is not connected to belief.

If one feels wonder at things that can be explained, one is able to see the miracle beyond the miracle. If one can only see wonder in the unexplained, one's wonder is dependent on the current gaps in human knowledge. Only when one has given up the need for wonder can one experience absolute wonder. As Wittgenstein said, this kind of wonder is not a wonder at the things that happen in the world, but is a wonder that there is a world at all.[1]

What the previous section said about *safe* can also be said about *wonder*. Having wonder normally makes sense only in situations when one is able to make a comparison between what one is unusually impressed by and situations where one is not usually impressed. I may wonder or marvel at the Grand Canyon but that is because during the course of my life I have only seen smaller and less grand canyons. The comparison makes wonder possible.

Absolute wonder, on the other hand, is expressed as wonder at the world or at existence or that anything should exist at all.[2] This is how

---

1. Wittgenstein, *Lecture on Ethics*, 47–48.
2. Wittgenstein, *Lecture on Ethics*, 47–48.

54

Wittgenstein describes it. The pattern is the same as we have seen before. Circumstantial wonder is amazed at things in the world, and the amazement or wonder comes from an experience that makes other similar things comparatively insignificant. Absolute wonder is amazed *that* there is a world. Since it is impossible to compare the feeling of existence to the feeling of nonexistence or never existence, the wonder is not the result of a comparison. The kind of thing that absolute wonder is amazed at is not a thing at all. It is *everything*, and *everything* is not the name of a thing in existence. What absolute wonder wonders at provides the context that makes circumstantial wonder possible.

I have already described the problem with miracles as they are typically understood. The problem, as I see it, is that miracles either lack the ability to convince people about a religious claim or they impede the possibility of religious living. The typical understanding suggests that miracles serve as a kind of evidence but that the evidence is still dependent upon the right interpretation. This is another way of saying that for every miraculous claim, there needs to be an alternative, non-miraculous explanation. But this is not what believers usually claim about miracles. They usually claim that miracles are convincing and that the only people who are not convinced are somehow blinded. Sometimes they accuse unbelievers of being slaves to reason and of having unreasonable evidentiary standards. This is to be expected within the belief paradigm.

Since the rise of science, the belief paradigm also means that the examination of a miraculous claim inevitably comes in the form of a scientific investigation. Wittgenstein describes the hypothetical miraculous scenario where a man suddenly sprouts a lion's head and roars.[3] According to Wittgenstein, our response would be to examine the man in search of an explanation, and the second we committed ourselves to such an examination we would have eliminated the miraculous possibility such an event could have made possible. This is the evidential trap of the Third Catch. But more to the point, this kind of approach to miracles leaves wonder out altogether. Such an examination is committed to determining whether or not an alternative, non-supernatural explanation is possible. If the examiner sees no alternative evidence, then the supernatural explanation replaces wonder at the world with a kind of circumstantial wonder that is dependent on evidentiary gaps. If the examiner sees an alternative explanation, then people divide between the believer's supernatural explanation and the unbeliever's

3. Wittgenstein, *Lecture on Ethics*, 49.

naturalistic explanation, and we are right back to the weeping statue of Mary. Miracles that create circumstantial wonder are there because they contrast with what we normally expect to be the case. Since they violate what we normally expect to be the case, they fall suspect to David Hume's argument that it always makes more sense to doubt miraculous claims than to build one's faith upon them.[4]

As with Hume, whether miracles occur is beside the point. The point is that the liberated religious are able to experience absolute wonder, and absolute wonder is wonder that there is anything at all. It is seeing the miracle beyond the miracle. The debate over whether God created the universe in six days is a debate over whether the world is a circumstantial miracle that should inspire circumstantial wonder or a circumstantial accident that should only inspire circumstantial curiosity. In other words, it is a debate over explanations. Creationists, denying the fact that there are two creation stories in Genesis 1 and 2 and that this has been known since before Augustine's time, insist that Genesis includes not only a description of how the universe was created but also an explanation of how life came to be on earth. Sometimes a mattress of denial is actually named *denial*.

Scientists, on the other hand, having worked on disproving Darwin's theory of natural selection and being unable to do so, have been persuaded by many different converging areas of study that the big bang, star formation, and natural selection offer the best descriptions and explanations for why the universe and earth are as they are. In this instance, the universe is the crying statue. The liberated religious accept what for believers is the worst-case scenario: that science is getting it right or is at least on a reasonable path that will lead to better understanding, and that such understanding is disinterested in what human beings want to be the case. The liberated religious do not require the denial of any facts. Unlike unbelievers, though like many actual scientists, the liberated religious are filled with wonder that these facts are as they are. This wonder is not based upon comparing current understanding with former understandings or hypothetical understandings. This wonder is an attitude toward the facts, whatever the facts happen to be. The fact that there is a universe at all. To be sure, scientists are also prone to misusing language, especially when they couch their investigations as means to understanding why we are here or as explanations that give meaning to human life. This is not the creative misuse of language that the liberated religious employ when expressing wonder. It is

4. Hume, *Enquiry Concerning Human Understanding*, 104–6.

the confused misuse of language that mistakes circumstantial explanations for an absolute explanation. While there is a context for understanding the former, there is no context for making sense of the latter. If there were, what is absolute would be just another circumstance and the conditions for absolute wonder would not exist.

Though many other examples could be selected, I take Job 38–41 and Psalm 145 as scriptural examples of absolute wonder.[5] Absolute wonder is expressed by saying that God is unfathomable and unsearchable. Both are also filled with circumstantial wonder because there is not much to say when it comes to absolute wonder. In both cases, circumstantial wonder is expressed by amazement at things in existence rather than amazement at existence. This is perfectly understandable.

Imagine receiving a card from each of your two best friends. In one card, your friend writes in every spare inch of space and fills the card up with circumstantial examples of how much you mean to that friend. In the other card your friend writes one sentence, "No words can express how much you mean to me." The first card is an example of a circumstantial expression. The second card is an absolute or transcendent expression. Which card will you value most? In most cases, people prefer the first card because the writer took time, made an effort, and recalled specific examples of your meaningful relationship. In the second card, the friend could have dashed that out without much thought. It certainly did not require the time and effort. But what if the cards were combined? What if your first friend had included the line from your second friend's card at the end of that long list of details? I think that this is a stained-glass way of interpreting what is happening in Job and in the Psalms. To show the power of the absolute expression it is necessary to spend the time on the circumstantial expression and then declare that circumstantial expression as unsatisfactory. This is how one expresses absolute wonder or absolute gratitude. To fail to express the dissatisfaction is to commit the idolatry of believers trapped in the belief paradigm. To express satisfaction with dissatisfaction is to transgress the reason of unbelievers. To understand that this expression is neither a literal nor a metaphorical claim about something that exists beyond language, but is itself a precise expression using language, is to avoid the belief paradigm's commitment to the correspondence theory of truth.

5. "Great is the LORD, and greatly to be praised; his greatness is unsearchable" (Ps 145:3 NRSV).

Seventh Catch

You can only be grateful when you have nothing to be grateful for.

You can only be absolutely grateful when you have nothing to be grateful for. If you have something to be grateful for, gratitude is reasonable. If you have nothing to be grateful for, gratitude is unreasonable. You can only have absolute gratitude when there is no reason to have it.

Gratitude comes easily and naturally when you have plenty of good things in your life. Generating lists of good things in life is what we do on occasions like Thanksgiving. We are grateful for relationships, food, clothing, shelter, jobs, health, possessions, etc. We are grateful when all of Maslow's needs are satisfied in our lives. By now the reader is familiar enough with these ideas to recognize these as circumstantial parts of life. Circumstantial gratitude is aimed at such things. As in all the other values I have discussed in this work, the circumstantial approach or need is vitally important and necessary for life. I hope to never denigrate the importance of any circumstantial attitude or need. Without circumstantial gratitude, we are ungrateful for the good things in life. Being ungrateful is a characteristic of petty, small people. At best, it is a phase that comes between immaturity and maturity.

Of course, and you see this coming, as important as circumstantial gratitude is, it is not the same thing as absolute gratitude. Absolute gratitude is religious gratitude or transcendent gratitude. What makes absolute gratitude religious or transcendent is that it is not based on the good things that happen in life. If one has absolute gratitude, one's circumstantial list of thanksgivings could be empty, and yet one is grateful for life. Being grateful for life is the same as feeling safe no matter what happens or feeling wonder that there is anything at all. While absolute gratitude is untouched by the contingencies of life, it does influence the way one experiences those contingencies.

It is important to remember that those who enjoy good things in life should not be the ones who tell those who are circumstantially deprived that they should be absolutely grateful. This is an attitude that one can only claim for oneself. If your life is filled with circumstantial griefs and lacks circumstantial blessings, then it is perfectly reasonable for you to not feel gratitude for life. It is insensitive and thoughtless to say otherwise. However, the transcendent or religious life aims for absolute gratitude.

Absolute gratitude, like absolute wonder, is based on making a comparison that cannot be made legitimately. Just as absolute wonder depends on the fact that you cannot compare that anything exists at all with non-existence, absolute gratitude depends on the fact that you cannot compare your own personal existence with the idea that you may never have existed at all. This is the kind of gratitude that is explored in the classic movie *It's a Wonderful Life*. Absolute gratitude is an approach to life that says that it is better to have been born than never to have been born. This comparison cannot be made and yet the illegitimate making of it is what generates absolute gratitude.

Comparative or circumstantial gratitude is based not only on appreciating the good things that one has but also on counterfactual claims that things could have turned out worse than they have. This "could be worse" mentality is behind the parental admonition to be grateful for your plate of food when others go hungry. Again, it is very important to have this kind of gratitude. It reminds us that we do not control our fates as much as our individualistic, capitalistic culture would have us believe. Seeing good things as gifts is a mark of humility.

In contrast to the "could be worse" approach of circumstantial gratitude is the "worst-case scenario" of absolute gratitude. This approach says that regardless of how bad things get in life, one is still grateful for life. This is what makes absolute gratitude so difficult and why many cannot attempt it. For some, the circumstantial griefs of life are so terrible and heartbreaking that they cannot affirm that it is better to have lived than not. For these people, things could not be worse, and they cannot find gratitude in the midst of their worst-case scenario. Such people are not unreasonable or defective and should be met with compassion rather than judgment. Most people's gratitude is circumstantial. This is what makes absolute gratitude transcendent.

Absolute gratitude is one way of recognizing that life is gratuitous. There is no reason or purpose to life. Seeing life as gratuitous is to surrender the mattress that believes God has a plan for each individual. The idea that God has a plan or purpose for our lives is a strategy of theodicy, which tries not only to justify God, but to justify ourselves. If God has a plan for my life and I enjoy the comforts of privileged living, then God must have intended for me to have the wealth that I enjoy. Conversely, if you are poor but God has a plan for your life, then God must have intended for you to be poor, and I am relieved of any responsibility to help the circumstantial griefs in your life. Because we tend to take too much credit for the good results in our lives and place too much blame on bad results in other peoples's lives, absolute gratitude is a way of correcting this tendency by embracing the concept of luck. This is something Job learned, but his friends did not.

If I recognize that I am lucky, I will take a humble attitude toward the good things in my life. I am also more likely to help those who have been less lucky. Luck removes the illusion that life tends to give us what we deserve. Given the complexities of human interactions, there is very little chance that people are consistently rewarded based on merit or punished for their faults. This is not to say that we do not have some limited control over the outcomes of our lives. But this limited control has more to do with attitude than result. If I am poor I should probably buy into the idea that hard work and self-discipline may improve my life. This is not a sermon that privileged people can preach to the poor, however, because if you are not poor then you should have the attitude that your life has been incredibly lucky. I once heard Dr. Fred Craddock, who at the time was professor of preaching and New Testament at Candler School of Theology, say, "Something that is true when whispered might be a lie when shouted." Likewise, a message that is helpful coming from poor people may be harmful if it used by the rich to justify themselves and maintain the status quo.

Absolute gratitude also has a way of giving us perspective on how we spend our days. Beyond our basic needs of shelter, clothing, food, and friendship most of us spend our lives passing time. This likely means that for the privileged, a good portion of life is like a Rube Goldberg machine where we fill our days with unnecessary tasks and overly dramatic complications just to have something to do. When something goes wrong in our overly complicated and privileged lives, which is a virtual guarantee with Rube Goldberg machines, our complaints come across as shallow and glib. Those who spend their lives trying to meet their basic circumstantial needs would envy the problems most of us enjoy.

First Thessalonians exhorts us to be grateful in all circumstances.[1] This is patent nonsense. The word *gratitude* gets its sense from circumstantial blessings. It is precisely because it makes no sense to be grateful in difficult circumstances that absolute gratitude is religious or transcendent. It is reasonable to be grateful when circumstances are positive. It is unreasonable to be ungrateful in positive circumstances. It is non-reasonable to be grateful beyond circumstances. This is absolute gratitude.

Related to being grateful in all circumstances is the admonition to "pray without ceasing." While not a Catch-22 on its own, this idea of continual prayer is consistent with all the Catch-22s of *Zero Theology*. This is to say that prayer is not an instrument meant to satisfy a circumstantial need, and it is not a form of communication to a present but invisible god. Since one cannot literally "pray without ceasing," I suggest that prayer is a way of life. It is a way of life that chooses to see the circumstances that comprise life as parts of a larger plot that transcends life. This larger plot is a choice. The larger plot in *Zero Theology* is a narrative where the worst-case scenario is regarded as true, and liberated religious people attempt to respond to that circumstance with compassion, courage, wonder, and gratitude. Believers see prayer as a means to achieve circumstantial ends. Unbelievers agree. Where believers and unbelievers disagree is over the efficacy of prayer, not the concept of prayer. This is to be expected when both groups are defined by the belief paradigm. Both disagree with the liberated religious and that disagreement is over the concept.

In *Zero Theology,* prayer is to religious life as breathing is to physical life. It is not something one chooses to do at this or that point in time. However, it is something that can be cultivated intentionally. Just as controlled breathing enhances life, controlled gratitude, wonder, courage, and compassion enhance religious life. I am not saying that prayer can never have circumstantial content because such content is the stuff of life. I am saying that prayer can never be reduced to circumstantial expressions, nor should the circumstantial expressions be seen as instruments meant to alter

1. "Rejoice always, pray without ceasing, give thanks in all circumstances; for this is the will of God in Christ Jesus for you" (1 Thess 5:16–18 NRSV).

the conditions of the worst-case scenario. If those conditions are altered, religious living becomes impossible.

EIGHTH CATCH

You are damned if you do and damned if you don't.

The Eighth Catch describes the human condition as a tragedy not because our lives are controlled by fate but because our choices preclude the possibility of having the freedom to not cause pain. To see the human condition as a tragedy is to weep like a miraculous religious statue or to feel utterly forsaken by one's concept of a present and caring God. In *Zero Theology*, it is the theologian's job to put words to the tears and forsakenness rather than trying to convince people that the human condition is not really a tragedy at all.

The Eighth Catch does not promote a comforting theology, but it sets the trap that creates the possibilities of despair and transcendence. It is a descriptive claim that one can affirm regardless of one's religious proclivities. It is the description to which a theology responds. Before I give a theological response to the grief encountered in this catch, I will first describe why we are trapped within it. To do that I will introduce two concepts that are distinct but related. Those concepts are called *relational space* and *ethical space.*

Relational space describes the network or interconnected web that all human beings inhabit. I choose *relational space* as an analog to Wittgenstein's *logical space* because whereas logical space was a way of conceptualizing all possible relationships between propositions and facts in the potential world, relational space refers to all possible relationships between groups and individuals in the interconnected world.[1] Ethical space, on the

1. See Wittgenstein, *Tractatus Logico-Philosophicus.*

other hand, refers only to those relationships within the interconnected web for which an individual or community feels ethically responsible. This feeling of ethical responsibility refers only to those with whom the individual or community identifies as intentionally impacted by its actions or inactions.

Relational space is characterized by three conditions. The first two are spatial (the *space* in relational space). The first is radical or small-world interconnectivity. The second is the unpredictability of butterfly effects in systems that are radically interconnected. The third is the opportunity costs of inhabiting such an interconnected and unpredictable network within the limitations of time.

Because it is both intuitive and has been supported by research from people like Stanley Milgram and Mark Granovetter, radical interconnectivity is now commonly accepted, not as prophetic poetry or ethical argument but as sociological fact.[2] The connections that tie us together are illustrated in the game Six Degrees of Kevin Bacon, which is an example from what is known as small-world theory. This theory demonstrates that it typically does not require a high number of relationships to connect any two individuals. Each individual is a node in the network of human interconnectivity. Nodes are connected to each other through relationships.

One important implication of the small world of relational space is that individual nodes impact each other in both intentional and unintentional ways. Individual persons or nodes may stand in direct or indirect relationship with each other. Whether a relationship is direct or indirect is determined by whether nodes interact with or without intermediary nodes. This means that while there may be a correlation between close proximity and direct relationship, close proximity and direct relationship are not guaranteed. One individual node may be directly connected to another node on the other side of the world and only indirectly connected to a node across town. This is the way human relationships work.

Presumably, one might have more control in direct relationships. Experience, however, tells us that there is often a gap between intention and consequence even in the most direct relationships. Still, it is easier to conceive of the possibility that directness and control stand in closer relationship than indirectness and control, even if that closer relationship offers no guarantee. In indirect relationships, one is less able to target these less connected nodes with one's intentions even on those rare occasions

2. Barabási, *Linked*, 9–54.

when one is aware of which indirect nodes will be impacted. This inability to control the impact of one's intended actions and how this plays out in the web of relational space is described in what is known as the butterfly effect.

Though based on previous work by Henri Poincaré, the butterfly effect was first introduced by MIT meteorologist Edward Lorenz, in a 1972 talk at a meeting of the American Association for the Advancement of Science entitled "Predictability: Does the Flap of a Butterfly's Wings in Brazil Set Off a Tornado in Texas?"[3] The butterfly effect refers to the fact that even the slightest change in initial conditions can lead to significantly different outcomes. The fact that initial conditions in the real world can never be fully accounted for means that we can never be completely confident of any description, much less prediction. It is often thought, incorrectly, that every slight change generates dramatic consequences. Not all slight changes are equal, so some slight differences do not impact complex systems in significant ways. However, in relational space, as in weather patterns, we do not know which slight differences will prove consequential and which will not. For the purposes of Zero Theology, it is sufficient to accept the fact that any action *could* impact others in relational space and that the impact could be consequential, though in most cases, we will never know which action led to which consequence. In other words, each moment is a renewed set of initial conditions and each action may impact other nodes anywhere in the network.

That human beings are connected and that individual actions have both intended and unintended consequences on both intended and unintended targets has become what can almost be described as a basic belief where doubt is impossible to imagine. Unless one is a member of a native tribe living in isolation, most people understand the interconnectivity of human relationships. Granted, there are political forces that seek to deny this reality. The emphasis that some place on personal responsibility and isolationism leads them to conclude that we can retreat to a point where our actions do not impact any unintended targets, but even these ideas are reactions against the reality of interconnectivity. They are the ethical arguments of some within a culture wanting to contract or limit the boundaries of ethical space. These arguments have no impact on the descriptive reality of relational space. Even if we could retreat and become like an isolated tribe our actions would still have unintended consequences to both intended and unintended targets within our own tribe.

3. Motter and Campbell, "Chaos at Fifty."

Because we live in a radically interconnected and unpredictable web of relationships, every action we take incurs opportunity costs. Whenever you choose a particular option, you lose the ability to gain the benefits that could have come from choosing from a host of other options. In economics, opportunity costs are only considered important when one is making a choice between mutually exclusive alternatives. In the dynamic world of small-world interconnectivity and unpredictable butterfly effects, every action incurs opportunity costs. This is because in addition to the complexity of relational space, human beings also exist in time.

I can only spend the next minute in so many ways. Any way I choose to spend that minute precludes the possibility that I could spend it doing other things. It is in the minutes of time that people decide to get married, eat a hot dog, go for a walk, read a book, or visit a friend. All of these decisions incur opportunity costs. All of these decisions could impact others in the interconnected web. Some obviously do so (getting married or visiting a friend). Others potentially do so (going for a walk may mean missing an emergency phone call or cause an automobile accident). Every action, regardless of whether an impact is noted in the actual world, incurs the counterfactual costs of what may have happened had that time been utilized differently. This is to say that while an action I take in the privacy of my own home may play a necessary but insufficient part in a nonlinear causal nexus that leads to some actualized impact elsewhere, it always incurs the counterfactual opportunity costs that come with the limitations of time. I am unable to predict whether my private act will cause an impact in the actual world or not. If it does, I will probably not know what role my private act played in bringing about that impact. Interconnectivity, butterfly effects, and opportunity costs comprise much of what it means to be human. If one is prepared to doubt any of these things, one cannot make any claims about the nature of human relational life.

Because time is the medium in which interconnectivity, butterfly effects, and opportunity costs take place, the present is always a consequence of the past and a precursor of the future. We are who we are, what we are, and where we are because of when we are. Genealogies tell us how we came to be and they accentuate the contingencies of life. If my wife's father had died of the snakebite he received as a young boy, my wife would not exist and neither would my two children, nor any subsequent generations of the family I have in this timeline. If the movie It's a Wonderful Life tells us anything, it is that the actions taken or not taken within an individual's life also have butterfly effects in the lives of others. Therefore, all the butterfly effects resulting from the actions taken or not taken by my wife and children and subsequent family generations would also be erased.

What is not addressed in *It's a Wonderful Life* are the negative consequences of George Bailey's life that would have also been erased along with the positive consequences. Because of the realities of living in relational space, any action one takes results in positive and negative consequences. I allow the driver in the other car to merge in front of me as an act of kindness. That merger plays a necessary but insufficient role in creating a series of events that leads to a fatal accident three miles down the highway. This kind of complex causal chain is beyond doubt. This is why our legal system differentiates between ultimate and proximate causes. The reckless driver, if he were temporarily granted omnipotent hindsight, may offer the reasonable explanation that it was my allowing him to merge that ultimately caused the fatal crash, but our legal system would not justify his subsequent recklessness by blaming the accident on my prior act of politeness.

If we live in a world where positive and negative consequences flow from any action an individual node may or may not take, then we lack absolute freedom. We may have a limited freedom when it comes to intentional choices, but we lack freedom when it comes to controlling the consequences that result from those choices. This is why differing schools of ethics focus on different parts of the process with virtue and deontological ethics focusing on choices while consequentialist ethics focuses on results. Regardless of which ethical theory one prefers, the fact remains that each of us causes unintended pain to others, whether the causal connection is identifiable or not. When we focus on the suffering that human beings cause each other we are focusing on one kind of circumstantial grief. Taking into account that everyone who is born into the network of relational space already participates in the inherited circumstantial griefs caused by prior iterations of the causal web, no person can claim to be immune from the causal inheritance. Once in the system, each person or individual node also causes unintended circumstantial grief to others due to small-world interconnectivity, butterfly effects, and opportunity costs.

In such a world, theology can no longer trivialize sin as the intended unethical actions of individuals. Even though the Hebrew Scriptures occasionally describe unintentional sin (Lev 4–5; Num 15), they still construe it as a morally culpable act that rises to consciousness after the fact rather than as a consequence of inhabiting relational space. When we live in relational space, every action, regardless of intention, causes negative consequences to others. There are no perfect choices for anyone who inhabits relational space.

One distinction between relational and ethical space is based on the difference between the actual and the aspirational. If one were to describe all connections between human beings, what one would be describing is relational space. If one were to describe all the goals of a particular community's ethical space, that description would never match up with the description of relational space. This is because ethics is intentional and prescriptive rather than unintentional and descriptive. What constitutes any ethical set of prescriptions is determined by a particular contextual community, even if they wish to universalize their ethical prescriptions. The complete transformation of relational space into ethical space can never be more than an aspiration because human beings will never have complete control over all the consequences of their intentions. Relational space may become more like a particular ethical space if the community that defines that ethical space achieves political hegemony, but it will never become identical to it.

If we couch this tension between relational and ethical space in Christian religious terms, we would say that however much we may pray that the kingdom of God becomes a reality "on earth as it is in heaven," we will always be caught in what is sometimes called the "fully present but not yet." Because *ZeroTheology* is less concerned with circumstantial results than with living a kind of life in the midst of absolute and circumstantial grief, this inability to fully consummate the kingdom is embraced as a condition of religious living rather than as something that frustrates the desire of faith.

Individuals gain their ideas regarding the boundaries of ethical space from communities that define for them what ethical behavior looks like. For example, some make the rather dubious claim that the Hebrew ethical command to love one's neighbor (Lev 19:18) was most likely confined to neighbor Hebrews. If we grant this interpretation, which I do not, this would suggest that the ethical space of ancient Hebrews was restricted only to fellow Hebrews. From the broader perspective of the Hebrew Scriptures, one can trace a widening of ethical space that includes aliens and strangers. From the Christian perspective, a gradual development of expanding ethical space can be traced from those early origins, through the Hebrew prophets, the life and teachings of Jesus, to the expansion of the Christian church from Jewish clientele to Gentile clientele. Indeed, when Jesus lifted up the Samaritan as neighbor, he was transgressing a boundary of his community's ethical space, which is the same thing as widening the boundary.[4] Today, the potential expanding of ethical space is manifested in justice discussions about including people with nontraditional sexual or gender identifications. Throughout human history there has always been tension between those who wish to expand the boundary of ethical space and those who wish to restrict it.

The boundaries of relational space have been expanded over human history as our knowledge of the world and other cultures has increased. The boundaries of ethical spaces expand, contract, shift, emerge, or disappear depending on how individuals and communities adopt or drop ethical responsibility for other people. Relational space is comprised of many distinct but overlapping ethical spaces just as humanity is comprised of distinct but overlapping cultures and identities. In today's world, relational space is more settled and its boundaries more stable, while ethical spaces constantly change, compete, and shift. Sometimes people will argue that the realities of relational space demand a particular and global ethical space. Such arguments are subject to the criticism of committing the naturalistic fallacy.

Dr. Martin Luther King writes the following in his "Letter from a Birmingham Jail":

> We are caught in an inescapable network of mutuality, tied in a single garment of destiny. Whatever affects one directly affects all indirectly.[5]

If we take these sentences from Dr. King as a theological or ethical claim about how, given our interconnectedness, we ought to treat one another, then he can be criticized for committing the naturalistic fallacy. However, if we take these sentences as only descriptive rather than ethically prescriptive, then the fallacy disappears and no theological or ethical claim is being made. In Zero Theology, I make no straightforward theological claims about the world. However, I do take other claims into account when scientific or nonreligious claims provide the limiting framework in which theological creativity can take place.

Creativity flourishes when limitations are established. This is another way of saying that religious life flourishes when nonreligious claims are accepted as limiting factors. It is this acceptance of limitations that believers

---

4. Luke 10:25–37.

5. King, "Letter From a Birmingham Jail."

deny and why they place their faith in limitation-transgressing miraculous claims. Believers deny the truth of what they perceive to be competing scientific claims because acceptance would defeat their theological claims. On the other hand, unbelievers think that scientific claims completely fill the frame, leaving no room for meaningful religious claims. The Catch-22s of *ZeroTheology* avoid the denial of believers and utilize the reductionism of unbelievers in order to make creative noncompetitive claims that can only be couched as paradoxes. This is why the liberated religious are not bothered by science.

The distinction between relational space and ethical space will help us navigate an analysis of the difficult and nuanced concept that traditional theology has called Original Sin. On the one hand, Original Sin refers to the human condition of relational space, which is to say that it transcends moral or ethical choices made by individuals. On the other hand, Original Sin has been used by theologians to explain ethical space or why human beings frequently make bad choices or take bad actions. Original Sin is their attempt to show a causal connection between the damaged condition of humanity and the sinful actions of individuals.

I cannot imagine a better example of the trouble explanatory theology gets into than when it offers the explanation called Original Sin. Theology's overly moral emphasis has led to much damage due to its reliance on shame and degradation. The concept was invented to explain two primary problems that early Christian theologians faced. The first is the universal human problem of evil and suffering. Original Sin was designed as theodicy to explain why a loving God would create a world where evil and suffering are ubiquitous. The second problem was of Christian theology's own making and is linked to another explanation offered by early Christian theologians. That problem, generally stated, was to explain how such an evil and suffering-filled world could ever be redeemed or restored. More specifically, the problem was trying to explain why Jesus had to die in order to redeem that world. Both of these problems assume that theology is trying to explain the divine but inaccessible elephant in the room.

Since I have moved away from the divine elephant toward creatively talking about divine beetles in boxes, I can reflect on the profound possibilities Original Sin might offer the contemporary world while eschewing the theological explanations that gave it birth. This view is not a theological explanation but does try to accept the kind of description of the world that both believers and unbelievers inhabit. In this way, I make no straightforward theological claim. I only start with a description of the world that is likely to find widespread agreement. That description of the world is the idea of relational space that I have already proposed.

Relational space is the name of the interconnected network where people damage one another because they are in relationships characterized by small-world theory, butterfly effects, and opportunity costs. Relational space would exist with as few as two directly connected individuals, though that would be simpler than the increasingly complex interconnected world we share. Traditional theology has primarily focused on explaining the ubiquity of intentionally evil actions. For this reason, a survey of the history of the concept, from Augustine to contemporary theology, reveals that theology has centered on Original Sin as alienation from God and as belonging to a moral conceptual framework that offers an etiological explanation for why evil or suffering exists in the world. Whenever one reads theological reflections on Original Sin, one is bound to come across words or phrases like *alienation, temptation, freedom of the will,* and *need for restoration.* Theology is still trapped in the conceptual cage constructed by early theologians.

In *ZeroTheology*, I do not focus on intended evils, as I believe that the fields of psychology, evolutionary biology, game theory, and ethics offer the only explanations that can be offered. By getting theology out of the explanation business, I do not need to concern myself with why we have ego needs that drive us to selfish, greedy, or evil actions. It is not that I find these characteristics of human behavior uninteresting or unimportant; I just do not see how morality-centered or etiologically driven theology helps advance our understanding in any way. When theology tries to explain why human beings are evil, it makes a claim that drives a divisive wedge between believers and unbelievers. The liberated religious do not need any such explanation from theology. In fact, the liberated religious suspect that the notion of evil itself has more to do with the conditions of relational space than the inner dispositions of its inhabitants. This does not deny that people may have dispositions that we label as evil; it simply asserts that those labels are themselves based on the interconnected communal construction of concepts.

It is tempting to try to understand where traditional theology went wrong. In fact, I will offer one possible explanation for how we got to where we are. However, I do not really wish to describe the Western theological path as wrong. I would prefer to say that it is no longer helpful. I am not sure there were other viable options given the historical realities that permeated the world when Christianity was first developing. Like the butterfly effect, small and possibly harmless decisions that impacted the early conditions of Christian theological development may have led to the present problematic conclusions that need to be eliminated in order to escape the belief paradigm.

Though there were certainly significant theological contributions from patristic theologians like Tertullian, Origen, and Irenaeus, I take Augustine to be the paradigmatic theologian who most set the trajectory of Christian thinking, and I believe that it is his conceptual spell that we most need to escape. That spell is cast in passages like the following: "Their nature was deteriorated in proportion to the greatness of the condemnation of their sin, so that what existed as punishment in those who first sinned, became a natural consequence in their children."[6] There is a name for this spell that can be retroactively applied to Augustine. It comes from psychology and is called correspondence bias or fundamental attribution error.

When early theologians looked at the world around them, they saw much the same world that we see when we look around us. They saw pain and suffering. They were less aware than we are of how radical interconnectivity, butterfly effects, and opportunity costs explain that pain and suffering. They were aware, however, that human beings struggle with the kinds of things that comprise the seven deadly sins. Each of us struggles with lust, gluttony, greed, sloth, wrath, envy, and pride despite our best efforts to eliminate them from our lives. When looking for proximate causes of most identifiable suffering in the world, early theologians were able to locate them in individual weaknesses that manifested themselves in one or more of the seven deadly sins. Early Christian theologians did not have the benefit of psychology, evolutionary biology, game theory, and secular ethics at their disposal so they proposed an explanation based on theology of the gaps. Since they lacked any other potential explanations for why human beings struggle with weaknesses that result in circumstantial griefs, they concluded that it must be because there is something wrong with human beings. They turned to a theological anthropology to explain an ultimate cause that would later be better explained by other nonreligious vocabularies. They decided there was a problem, and the problem, because of its apparent universality and tenacity, must exist at the dispositional level within each individual.

6. Augustine, *City of God*, 413–14.

This dispositional explanation raised a problem for Christian theologians. Why would a good and loving God create something with such a dispositional flaw? This is the impetus toward theodicy that drives the traditional notion of Original Sin. In order to avoid assigning blame to a loving Creator God, they had to locate the source of the dispositional flaw in a free individual human action rather than in the way God designed human beings. The assumption was that human communities are simply collections of autonomous individuals and that any flaws in the system can be traced to flaws in the individuals who inhabit that system. Because Augustine believed theology's task was to explain the etiological origins of evil, it was important that all humanity's flaws be traced back to a single and original actor. Regardless of how much merit one places in the contemporary application of correspondence bias or fundamental attribution error, the traditional idea of Original Sin is an example of fundamental attribution error writ large.

Fundamental attribution error is the name given to the tendency of human beings to ascribe other people's bad behavior to flawed dispositions rather than to the situations or contexts in which those other human beings operate. Of note is that we tend to do this to other people but not ourselves. For example, if a driver cuts me off in traffic I am more likely to conclude that the driver is a jerk than to conclude that the driver must have a justified reason to be in a hurry. However, when I am the driver who cuts someone off, I justify my behavior by appealing, not to my disposition, but to my circumstances. I had to cut you off because I am running late for a job interview and other drivers have been slowing me down all morning. I am a good person who had to do an unfortunate thing. We also extend this personal exemption from dispositional judgment to close friends and relatives with whom we identify when they tell us of occasions where they had to act like jerks. Another way of saying this is to say that the more we understand the situation or context that motivates what is normally perceived as negative behavior, the more likely we are to excuse or pardon that bad behavior by appealing to the situation or context. The less we understand the surrounding circumstances the more likely we are to judge bad behavior as indicative of the actor's evil disposition.

The traditional notion of Original Sin exhibits all of the characteristics of fundamental attribution error except one. When theologians ascribed negative or sinful behaviors to the flawed dispositions of individuals they included themselves among the bad actors. I think they did this because they were trying to explain the human condition from God's perspective. No clearer example of this self-identification with fundamental attribution error can be seen than the famous section from Paul in Romans 7:13–25.[7] These words from Paul sound like the testimony of someone at an addiction-recovery support group. We understand addiction as a nonethical human frailty; early Christian theologians did not have that concept in their vocabulary.

There are two scriptural texts that lie behind the traditional theological concept of Original Sin. The first is the Garden of Eden story found in Genesis 2:15—3:21 and the second is Paul's interpretation of that story found in Romans 5:12–21. For the purpose of this section, I provide the reader with a portion of the Romans text:

> Therefore, just as sin came into the world through one man, and death came through sin, and so death spread to all because all have sinned—sin was indeed in the world before the law, but sin is not reckoned when there is no law. Yet death exercised dominion from Adam to Moses, even over those whose sins were not like the transgression of Adam, who is a type of the one who was to come.[8]

As Paul makes clear, he sees the Garden of Eden story as an etiological explanation of how sin entered the world. Included in this etiology is an explanation of death. Death was a preoccupation of early Christian thinkers. They expected God to provide explanations for all theological questions. They did not see that it is the fact of death that makes religious life possible. Death is not necessarily a bad thing that needs explanation or justification.

7. "Did what is good, then, bring death to me? By no means! It was sin, working death in me through what is good, in order that sin might be shown to be sin, and through the commandment might become sinful beyond measure. For we know that the law is spiritual; but I am of the flesh, sold into slavery under sin. I do not understand my own actions. For I do not do what I want, but I do the very thing I hate. Now if I do what I do not want, I agree that the law is good. But in fact it is no longer I that do it, but sin that dwells within me. For I know that nothing good dwells within me, that is, in my flesh. I can will what is right, but I cannot do it. For I do not do the good I want, but the evil I do not want is what I do. Now if I do what I do not want, it is no longer I that do it, but sin that dwells within me. So I find it to be a law that when I want to do what is good, evil lies close at hand. For I delight in the law of God in my inmost self, but I see in my members another law at war with the law of my mind, making me captive to the law of sin that dwells in my members. Wretched man that I am! Who will rescue me from this body of death? Thanks be to God through Jesus Christ our Lord! So then, with my mind I am a slave to the law of God, but with my flesh I am a slave to the law of sin" (Rom 7:13–25 NRSV).

8. Rom 5:12–14 NRSV.

It is as if they are asking, "God, why did you put death in the game?" and expecting God to explain or justify the decision. For *Zero Theology*, such explanations or justifications are unnecessary. Death is one of the conditions that make religious life possible. If we remove the conditions, we remove the possibility of religious living.

Paul does not share *Zero Theology*'s acceptance of limiting conditions as necessary for religious living, and like most theologians, he wants to explain them in hopes of escaping them. Like many contemporary theologians, Paul is aware that there is a distinction between the concept of sin and the concept of morality, though he sees a necessary overlap. He makes his awareness clear when he writes, "Sin was indeed in the world before the law, but sin is not reckoned when there is no law." If we take Paul at his word, then he distinguishes sin from moral transgression because moral transgression can only occur when there is a moral law to transgress. If Original Sin is a condition that preexisted moral law, then it makes no sense to speak of its advent into the world as the result of a moral transgression. This distinction between sin and moral transgression is somewhat reflected in my distinction between relational space and ethical space. The difference is that relational space requires no etiological explanation. It is simply "there like life" or "where two or three are gathered."[9]

Theologians have felt that the conditions of human life do require an etiological explanation, and they have attempted to find it in the second chapter of Genesis. Unfortunately, they put more weight on the story than it can bear. First, we need to notice that the conditions in the Garden of Eden are not like any world we can inhabit or imagine. When God placed Adam and Eve into the garden, it was a premoral or preethical world. We know this because in the garden there was a tree called the Tree of the Knowledge of Good and Evil and if Adam and Eve ate of its fruit they would become morally knowledgeable. God commanded them not to eat of its fruit and threatened them with the punishment of death if they did so. This story, at it is presented, is a narrative example of what is known in logic as begging the question. Unlike its popular usage, where begging the question has come to mean a scenario or explanation that provokes further questioning, begging the question originally referred to the logical fallacy where the conclusion of an argument is assumed in one of its premises. In the Garden of Eden story, at least as it has been interpreted by Christian theologians, the conceptual components of the moral world are present prior to the

9. Wittgenstein, *On Certainty*, 73; and Matt 18:20.

introduction of morality into the story. In other words, the meaning of the story trades on the very concepts that it is supposed to introduce.

Consider the following concepts that we find prior to Adam and Eve eating of the tree of moral knowledge. We encounter a divine command to be obedient, a threat of death if disobedient, a description of something called "good and evil" located in the fruit of a particular tree, and the temptation to eat of that fruit. The concepts *command, obedience/disobedience, threat,* and *temptation* would have been unknown to and impossible for Adam and Eve to conceive of if the conditions in Eden are as otherwise described in the story and as early theologians like Augustine took them to be. The concept of command, and its associated concept of obedience/disobedience, would make no sense in a premoral world. In order to understand that obedience is moral and disobedience immoral, Adam and Eve would have already had to eat of the fruit of the tree of morality. In order to understand God's threat of punishment, Adam and Eve would have needed previous experience of being threatened and would have needed to understand that the punishment is a consequence of an immoral act. In a world lacking the concept of morality and its associated concepts of reward and punishment, threat would have been unintelligible. In a world where death was unknown and never experienced, the specific threat of death would have had little meaning. Of all concepts that beg the question, however, the notion of *temptation* is the most egregious example. It is simply impossible for Adam and Eve to experience temptation apart from already participating in a moral world. In a premoral world, temptation would be more like *stimulus*, which completely lacks moral connotations.

There are two significant truths that can be derived from this conceptual analysis of the Eden story. The first is that it is logically impossible for a moral world to envision a premoral world and account for the introduction of morality into that world where a moral action is the means of introduction. The examination of cultural evolution may be able to describe how notions of morality developed, but that description would not include the very moral judgments it is meant to explain. The second truth is that this story is not accidental mythology—meaning that it could have happened that way but did not. This story is necessarily mythological; it could never have happened as described. This is important because it means that even if we lacked other creation myths both in and out of scripture, which we do not, this creation story could not be historical. Even if we lacked nonreligious accounts of our origins, which we do not, this story could not be historical. The classic interpretation of this creation myth assumes that human beings could be created in an instant with entire conceptual frameworks intact.

By forgetting the communal and conceptual requirements that would be needed to make the Garden of Eden story intelligible, traditional theologians were able to insert assumptions of individual autonomy. Such a path inevitably leads to a dispositional analysis where the central themes are disobedience, alienation, freedom of the will, and potential restoration. By gazing inward at human souls rather than outward at the human situation of relational space, theologians limited their explanatory options. Of course, their explanatory options were already limited when they sought theological explanations instead of sociological or psychological explanations. In other words, by locating the problem deep in the interior of the human soul, theologians chose an unknown fuzzy place where theological speculation could abound unchecked.

The impossibility of the Eden myth does not render it useless for theological creativity in *Zero Theology*. In fact, once the story is approached as an imaginary *as if* rather than as a claim to be believed or denied, new possibilities emerge that may have much to offer modern life at the close of the belief paradigm. If we inhabit the story we begin to see something that interpreters devoted to theological explanation may have missed.

I believe that if we focus on a feature of the Adam and Eve story that has hitherto been ignored, we can free ourselves from the dispositional conceptual trap. Augustine framed our self-understanding of what it means to be human and used that understanding to interpret the Adam and Eve story. This self-understanding, inherited from earlier philosophers, particularly Plato, is that human beings are primarily rational agents. The rational and the agential identifications stand together, for if we lacked agency, rationality would be useless and if we lacked rationality, agency would be inaccessible. That is why Augustine, and theologians ever since, have focused on the concepts that comprise rational agency. These concepts are freedom of the will, temptation, and intentional disobedience. To break out of this conceptual framework, I would like to make two further observations about the Adam and Eve story.

The first is that in eating from the tree of moral knowledge Adam and Eve were *trying* to be something that they already were. They were told that they would be "like God" despite the fact that they were already made in the divine image. This "attempt" is consistent with rational agency's self-understanding. The concept of attempt plays a significant role in the conceptual matrix of rational agency. If we subtract it, we lose concepts associated with it. These other concepts include intention, criteria (success/failure), pride/shame. Premoral Adam and Eve knew nothing of the concept of attempt. They had never experienced success or failure, never utilized criteria to judge, and never felt pride or shame until after eating from the Tree of the Knowledge of Good and Evil. In order for the concept of attempt to be intelligible, the attempted goal must be something that may or may not be attained. If one already is what one is attempting, one cannot be said to try.

The concept of attempt or try is also one of those tricky concepts that can get lost in infinite regress. It makes sense to say that I am trying to live a moral life but it makes no sense to say that I am *trying to try* to live a moral life. The problem with the concept of attempt is that it can always be added to any human activity regardless of the context. If I am shooting basketball, someone can say that I am trying to shoot basketball. If I am taking a nap someone can say I am trying to take a nap. When Adam and Eve ate of the tree of knowledge, theologians say that they were trying to be what they already were, which is to suggest that they were moral attempters before they could possibly understand either morality or attempt. If you attempt to become an attempter, you are trying to try. When the story is interpreted as an etiological story about the introduction of sin through the act of disobedience, the lack of moral conceptual possibility is ignored and we are told that when Adam and Eve disobeyed God, they were trying to try to be like God. I would suggest that this interpretation reveals that when it comes to morals or ethics, traditional theology defines human beings as attempters. By defining ourselves as moral attempters we see ourselves as human doers rather than as human beings. Whenever one attempts being, one can only fail at doing. According to the traditional interpretation, this is what happened to Adam and Eve.

The second point I wish to make relies on my previous observation that Adam and Eve could not be tempted prior to the advent of a moral conceptual framework. This is because one does not move from being a human being to a human doer by means of temptation. Temptation belongs only to the land of human doers. Where one can attempt an action, one can be tempted to attempt that action. Where one cannot make an attempt, one cannot fathom being tempted to make it. Prior to the advent of the moral conceptual framework, Adam and Eve would have been closer to animals responding on instinct or reacting to stimuli than our contemporary understanding of what it means to be human. While a dog may make an effort in order to escape a fence, the dog does not conceive of that effort as an attempt. The dog is not trying to escape because the dog knows nothing of criteria, which includes the notions of success and failure. However, we find it difficult to express what we see the dog doing without using the concept of attempt with which we are so familiar: "Look at that dog trying to get out of that yard." I believe that this same tendency is what led Augustine and other theologians to create the dispositional-based, moral, rational-agent interpretation of the Adam and Eve story and the subsequent narrative that constitutes traditional Western theology.

Regarding human beings as moral attempters was only the first part of the dispositional narrative. The other significant piece is that human beings are flawed moral attempters as a result of Adam and Eve's sin. As almost all students learn in seminary, the earliest concept of sin was based on the notion of missing the mark. This missing of the mark already contains all the necessary conceptual presumptions that give rise to the autonomous rational agent. In order to miss the mark one has to have an intention to hit the mark, make a deliberative attempt to hit the mark, and understand what counts as hitting the mark. When a naïve ethics focuses on isolated actions it can seem that ethical decisions are as simple as hitting the desired target. This is to ignore the interconnected and uncontrollable aspects of relational space. The ethical target is defined by the community in which the individual resides. The community sometimes decides whether the individual has hit or missed the mark if the individual is unable to do that for him or herself.

The traditional notion of Original Sin went further and stated that the reason all individuals miss the moral target, which it defined as obedience or right relationship with God, must be because their targeting system is flawed. This flaw flowed from Adam and Eve's original sin. According to Augustine, and theologians who followed him, this flawed targeting system was the fallen condition of human beings and was passed down from generation to generation. In order to avoid the flawed ethical targeting system, Jesus was born of a virgin so as to bypass the sexual reproductive act responsible for passing down the dispositional flaw. Of course, if Jesus did not have the dispositional flaw, we cannot claim that he was "tempted like we are."[10]

10. "For we do not have a high priest who is unable to sympathize with our weaknesses, but we have one who in every respect has been tested as we are, yet without sin"

79

Now that I have addressed how the story of Eden could not be an etiological explanation regarding how sin entered into the world and have shown that Adam and Eve could not have been tempted since they lacked the concept of attempt, it is time to state what I regard as a very important but previously unrealized fact about Original Sin. Where temptation is not possible, conviction is not possible. Original Sin did not enter the world through an act of temptation and cannot be removed from the world through an act of conviction. This understanding of Original Sin is like my concept of relational space and unlike traditional theology's equation of Original Sin with a dispositional flaw.

Normally, I am not tempted to force poor people into sweatshop labor conditions when I consider purchasing clothing that was made in a sweatshop. There are conditions where this temptation could arise. If I am involved in a direct relationship with poor workers and have the ability to exploit them for personal gain, I may be tempted to exploit them or convicted to stop exploiting them. That is because I may come to see them as co-people in ethical space. When I am in an indirect relationship with the workers and know nothing about the causal chain that connects my purchase with their exploitation, there is no temptation. This is a relational space problem. Should someone make the causal connection clear to me, those workers could enter into my ethical space and I may now be tempted or convicted regarding my clothing purchases. But having someone make the causal connection clear to me is not a case of someone convicting me of a sin; it is the case of someone informing me about a relational-space connection of which I was unaware. Adam and Eve could not have been tempted by the serpent in the garden because they lacked the conceptual framework necessary to experience temptation. The serpent informed them about a situation in relational space: "When you eat of the fruit your eyes will be opened and you will be like God."[11] This is the same as someone pointing out the causal chain between my purchasing decisions and the exploitation of poor people. My eyes are opened and an ethical choice becomes possible.

When our eyes are opened to the realities of suffering in relational space we frequently feel abandoned by the God of our particular community's ethical space. According to the serpent, becoming like God in Genesis 3 referred to having God's knowledge of good and evil. When we become

---

(Heb 4:15 NRSV).

11. Gen 3:5 NRSV.

aware that because the conditions of relational space are as they are, that pain will be caused even if every individual acted with the purest and most ethical intentions, we may become paralyzed by such knowledge. This movement toward the morally silent God of relational space is actually a move away from the morally loud God proclaimed by our particular ethical space. To be fully aware of the realities of relational space is to be forsaken by your ethical sense of the divine and the potential of divine rescue. It is based on this awareness that I choose to reinterpret one of Jesus's statements at his crucifixion. When Jesus says, "My God, my God, why have you forsaken me?"[12] he is tearfully responding to the human condition of inhabiting relational space.

Each party present at the crucifixion is fulfilling the goals of whatever ethical space that party inhabits. The Jewish leaders are looking out for the safety of their own people and realize the danger from Rome whenever a messianic pretender presents himself. The Romans are doing what governments do. They are punishing those who would seek to replace them with another form of rule. It is immaterial whether contemporary Christians think that Rome was mistaken and that the Jewish leaders are the villains in the story. If we were able to ask each party at the crucifixion why they were doing what they were doing, they would each have an ethical argument to make. The truth of relational space is that even if all people believe they are attempting to do the right thing, innocent people will suffer. When Jesus realizes this on the cross he fully expresses the human condition. To know what it means to be human is to feel Godforsaken, which is to confront the reality of absolute grief in the face of an absent and silent God. To respond expressively to this reality should be theology's goal. When Jesus cried out about being forsaken, he was doing theology.

When one combines the conditions of relational space, which includes small-world interconnections, butterfly effects, and opportunity costs, one understands that any action or decision, including not acting or not deciding, creates pain and suffering and that this is true regardless of an individual's intentions. For these reasons, another way of conceiving Original Sin is to see it as a theological version of what our legal system calls public welfare offenses or strict liability offenses. These are offenses that do not require bad intentions in order to convict a person of wrongdoing. According to Joshua Dressler,

12. Matt 27:46; Mark 15:34 NRSV.

> With the advent of the Industrial Revolution, legislatures found it necessary to deal with a new problem: conduct by a single actor that, although not morally wrongful, could gravely affect the health, safety, or welfare of a significant portion of the public.[13]

It is easy to see how this quotation mirrors much of the suffering that is caused by conditions in relational space. Dressler further states that what the Industrial Revolution created was a need to distinguish crimes that are *malum in se* (inherently wrongful) from crimes that are *malum prohibitum* (wrong because it is prohibited).[14] This distinction is mirrored in the scriptural distinction between intentional and unintentional sins and in the theological distinction between sin as a committed act and Original Sin as the condition that renders sinful acts unavoidable.

In the legal system, persons who are convicted for these public-welfare or strict-liability offenses are usually not stigmatized or punished severely because the crime did not make them morally culpable, even though it made them legally responsible. This distinction between moral culpability and legal responsibility is important when thinking of the conditions of relational space. In relational space, our interconnectivity, inability to control consequences, and the opportunity costs of any human action means that where an individual's action causes unintended harm, that person is responsible as a member of the social network, but not morally culpable as a bad actor. When Augustine and Christian theologians succumbed to blaming a dispositional flaw for suffering and evil, they were committing themselves to an individual or dispositional *malum in se* interpretation of sin and eliminating the possibility of public-welfare or strict-liability interpretations that are *malum prohibitum* and bear no signs of moral culpability.

When Augustine holds individuals responsible for isolated evil actions, he is not that dissimilar from his opponent, Pelagius. However, when Augustine describes sin as something that the individual is born into or inherits, he is at odds with Pelagius because he moves closer to something like strict-liability, public-welfare offenses. Pelagius would have hated thinking of sin as belonging to a strict-liability web that no individual could escape. But he would have hated it because he assumed a stigma and a severe penalty as punishment. Where the stigma or any external punishment is removed, the problem of conceptualizing sin as a nonmoral but inevitable attribute of relational space is also removed. This removal also eliminates the great

---

13. Dressler, *Understanding Criminal Law*, 145.
14. Dressler, *Understanding Criminal Law*, 145.

moral or dispositional stain that Augustine took as explanation for why human beings commit evil actions and with which Pelagius disagreed so passionately. In *Zero Theology*'s relational space, neither Augustine nor Pelagius would be completely satisfied, though each would be partially correct.

Time and again, I have proposed that theological explanation is theology at its worst. I have also suggested that theology would be better conceptualized as a kind of poetry that responds to the conditions of the world. Until now, I have left these statements hanging, issued them as proclamations. At this point, however, I believe it important to describe why I think theology goes astray when it wanders into explanation and what I mean when I say that it ought to be more like poetry. As you may expect by this point, I turn to Wittgenstein for assistance. In doing so, I will return once again to the relative/absolute value distinction he made in his *Lecture on Ethics*, but I will start with a few comments from his *Philosophical Investigations*:

> Words are connected with the primitive, the natural, expressions of the sensation and used in their place. A child has hurt himself and he cries; and then adults talk to him and teach him exclamations and, later, sentences. They teach the child new pain behavior.[15]

Here Wittgenstein is talking about how words are learned for certain natural expressions and then used in place of those expressions. When thinking of natural expressions, I imagine things like cries, sighs, grunts, laughs, and so on. Parents are aware of this phenomenon and evoke it whenever they say to a crying or screaming child, "Use your words!" The words are not synonymous with the expressions they replace, but they build upon them as they expand the range of possible communication. They provide information that the expression does not. A cry does not indicate where it hurts or how the pain came to be. A patient who only screams at the doctor is unlikely to receive effective treatment. *On the other hand, such words are not always a report meant to convey information.* Sometimes they are substitutes for a cry, sigh, grunt, or laugh. I suggest that when doing theology, we should regard words as substitutes for basic human expressions, particularly expressions that are responding to grief. This would be like poetry. When we talk about doing theology, we should remember that our words should always retain some of their expressive function, even as we are conveying thoughts, critiques, and information.

15. Wittgenstein, *Philosophical Investigations*, 89.

Grief, whether absolute or circumstantial, is first and foremost a primitive cry. When believers assume that theology is primarily about information conveyance or explanation and forget that it is undergirded by a primitive cry, their theological language serves as a distancing mattress. As an example, consider the difference between these two translations of Romans 8:22–23:

> We know that the whole creation has been groaning in labor pains until now; and not only the creation, but we ourselves, who have the first fruits of the Spirit, groan inwardly while we wait for adoption, the redemption of our bodies. (NRSV)

> All around us we observe a pregnant creation. The difficult times of pain throughout the world are simply birth pangs. But it's not only around us; it's *within* us. The Spirit of God is arousing us within. We're also feeling the birth pangs. These sterile and barren bodies of ours are yearning for full deliverance. (The Message)

I was fortunate enough to have had a conversation with Fred Craddock some years ago. As mentioned previously, Dr. Craddock was an extremely influential preaching professor at Emory University's Candler School of Theology. He was also a delightful man. The conversation took place at a preaching workshop he offered to about eight clergy near his home in north Georgia. Dr. Craddock had us read various translations of Romans 8:22–23 and discuss their differences. I do not recall which translations we read but the two I have cited from the New Revised Standard Version (NRSV) and The Message will suffice to make my point.

I would argue that, in this particular case, the NRSV does a better job of staying connected to the primitive expression behind the passage than does The Message. In the NRSV, one can hear the groaning in the text. It is as though you are in the room during delivery. In contrast, The Message sounds like someone giving a report about what is happening in the delivery room. The NRSV feels more expressive. The Message feels more informative. At the workshop, I took Dr. Craddock to mean that getting to the real feeling of the text better prepares the preacher to connect that feeling with the congregation. This would also remind the preacher that being religious is not primarily an intellectual exercise. I do not suggest that the NRSV consistently stays closer to feeling or that The Message consistently distances feeling, only that they do so in this particular case. I will also point out that in my experience, mainline progressive Christians tend to prefer translations that distance feeling. I think this corresponds to an addiction mainline progressive Christians have to informative or explanation-based theology.

When I criticize theological explanation, I do so with the view that theology should be rooted in human expressive responses. This is why I have said that theology or faith is a response to the limiting conditions of life rather than an explanation of those limiting conditions that promises escape. The relative/absolute value distinction made by Wittgenstein draws from that same perspective. Having absolute wonder at the world is rooted in a feeling. Absolute safety is a feeling. This is not to say that theology is only expressive. If it were only expressive I would not need to do the kind of conceptual analysis I have offered in this book. What we say is very important. Absolute wonder and absolute safety require a conceptual or linguistic leap that allows the speaker to express feelings and attitudes in a transcendent way. This transcendent usage is not the normal usage of straightforward claims that can be judged as reasonable or unreasonable. Theology, when it is functioning at its best, stays connected with the expressions that lie beneath it, and uses those expressions to give life to a language that does not lead us astray with explanations or justifications. I try to accomplish this in *ZeroTheology* through the Catch-22s and by placing the human experience and expression of absolute grief at both the beginning and end of the religious journey. This does not discount other experiences and expressions such as joy or wonder or love. However, I maintain that as long as absolute grief is not confronted, our experiences of joy or wonder or love are likely built on mattresses of denial that prevent us from experiencing and expressing the full range of human life.

While there have been occasional references to the positive effects that occur in relational space, most of what I have focused on to this point has emphasized the negative. Individuals, through no fault of their own, regardless of noble intentions, cause harm to other individual nodes in the interconnected web. But the positive aspects of relational space cannot be ignored. In order to discuss how relational space can be both positive and negative and how significant this feature is in understanding Original Sin, I need to talk about the importance of what I call *converse synonyms*.

Converse synonyms refer to words that produce the same effects despite the fact that their usage is shaded by an oppositional evaluative tone. Recognizing converse synonyms is a way of breaking out of traps and gaining a fresh perspective on an all too familiar conceptual landscape. Rooted in the notion of converse synonyms is the idea that one can use positive or negative expressions in order to bring about similar results. The lifeguard may shout "Don't run!" to kids who are running around the pool. That same lifeguard could also shout "Walk!" to achieve the same results. In practical life, a lifeguard probably gets better results by using each expression unpredictably.

Converse synonyms are more complex than the lifeguard's simple commands. They typically play a role of making a distinction between something that is morally praiseworthy and something that is worthy of condemnation. I can think of no better or purer example of converse synonyms than *blame* and *credit*. Reduced to their most essential definitions, both words could be defined as "giving attribution to" or "assigning responsibility for." To blame someone is to say that he is responsible for a negative result: "I blame him for the drowning." To credit someone is to say that she is responsible for a positive result: "I give her credit for saving his life." This is the normal way these words are used. But consider the jarring effect of reversing them. "I blame her for saving his life," and "I give him credit for the drowning." Though jarring, this reversal is sensible. One can imagine a context where someone might say these very sentences. This is because *blame* and *credit* are converse synonyms, though we typically choose one when we are feeling negative and the other when feeling positive.

I have already stated that the lack of temptation is one of the defining features of Original Sin and that most of the harm we cause one another in relational space is not the result of temptation. I have also stated that if one does not enter into a sin through temptation, one will not exit that sin through conviction. This is because *temptation* and *conviction* are another example of converse synonyms. Each word refers to an inducement to change a moral or immoral activity into its moral opposite. Temptation can be defined as the inducement to commit an unethical act or to stop committing an ethical act. Conviction can be defined as the inducement to stop committing an unethical act or to start committing an ethical act. Like blame and credit, these terms can be reversed. We know this because we can make sense of "He was tempted to do the right thing." "He was convicted to stop doing the right thing" is an equally sensible sentence.

In stating that these converse synonyms can be shown when their roles are reversed I am only stating that such reversals are sensible, not that they are identical. If they were identical they would not be *converse* synonyms, they would just be synonyms. In fact, in most cases, examples of converse synonyms deployed in their reversed settings will strike us as jarring. This jarring impact is precisely the reason for using them, however. When we reverse the converse synonyms so that each occupies its opposite evaluative field, we help ourselves notice things about our concepts that typically go unnoticed. Converse synonyms provide a shift in perspective that may reveal the hidden opposite connotation that the usual term normally conceals. In addition to blame/credit and temptation/conviction, other examples may include threat/promise and dread/hope.

The reason for this detour into converse synonyms is that it creates the perfect place to approach the flipside of the Eighth Catch. This flipside converts Original Sin into Original Grace and suggests that in this usage, sin and grace are converse synonyms. This would mean that contrary to theologians who are preoccupied with morality and etiology, Original Sin is simply a way of describing the conditions of human interconnectedness in relational space. Original Grace describes the very same thing. Original Sin and Original Grace stand together in the same way that blame/credit and temptation/conviction do. When we realize this, we understand that the Eighth Catch can be rephrased as:

You are good if you do and good if you don't.

This is the traditional theological expression of divine grace. This new formulation is not a new catch; it states the same thing as the original catch, just from a converse perspective. However, though it communicates the same thing, the feeling is as different as a lifeguard shouting "Walk!" rather than "Don't run!"

For two thousand years, people have been so beat down with the overly moralistic and humiliating notion of Original Sin that they are tired of hearing it and inoculated against it. However, seeing Original Sin as a converse synonym for Original Grace may open people up to a more profound understanding of human life. But more importantly, one does not need to be a believer in order to embrace both sides of the Eighth Catch. In *Zero Theology*, Original Sin is destigmatized so that what it says about individual nodes in relational space can have descriptive power. This destigmatizing is also communicated by Original Grace. Just as the effectiveness of a lifeguard's commands depends on her ability to use the positive and negative versions in unpredictable ways, the power of Original Sin and

Original Grace rests on our ability to use them both rather than jettisoning the negative because of the traditional associations with blame and guilt.

If we return to Dr. King's statement about human connection, radical interconnectivity is about more than responsibility; it is also about empowerment. When living in a radically interconnected world comprised of butterfly effects and opportunity costs, individual nodes have the power to transform the system with small steps. Some of these steps can be taken strategically. This is the flipside of intentional bad actions that cause targeted harm. We will also be unable to control all of the consequences of our positive actions. Theologically, this has been expressed as the inability to earn one's way to salvation by doing good works. The challenge is to continue to try to expand ethical space even as we understand that no ethical space can ever overtake relational space. The futility of ultimate accomplishment is compensated by the liberated religious person's commitment to living a life that is its own reward. Individual nodes have all the power a node can have. Each has the power, but not the control, to affect change throughout the system. Each individual has the power to make transcendent choices when faced with the inescapable realities of living in relational space. Of course, some will feel defeated by these realities. It is to such people that I quote Paul, "Should we continue in sin in order that grace may abound? By no means!"[16] Paul asks and answers this right after giving his own version of the interplay between sin and grace. As I have already stated, one must risk despair to gain absolute peace. One must feel trapped before one can choose the transcendent life.

Original Grace destigmatizes the conditions of relational space by removing any trace of moral culpability for it. Given the conditions created by small-world connectivity, butterfly effects, and opportunity costs, no individual has access to perfect choices. One is always choosing from flawed alternatives because any choice causes negative effects or negative counterfactuals. Where there are no good choices, there can be no moral culpability. Where there are no good choices, arguments for absolute freedom of the will seem quaint and naïve. The conditions of relational space are the conditions that any social species inhabits if it lives in an interconnected world. It is not the result of a fall. As I have stated before, the conditions of relational space do not preclude the usual notion of intentional harmful acts and the volitional requirement demanded when judging such actions.

16. Rom 6:1b–2a NRSV.

I just do not see why theology should weigh in on matters that psychology, sociology, game theory, and secular ethics are better able to analyze.

When one inhabits relational space, or the conditions of Original Sin/Original Grace, one is trapped in the human being/human doer conundrum. Adam and Eve were beings who were tempted to be what they already were. They tried to be. One cannot attempt being. If we wish to speak of a fall, then the fall in Eden was from being to doing. Remember that Eden is necessarily mythological; there have never been any people we would call "human" who we would not also describe as doers. Whether we describe early humans as hunter-gatherers or as nomadic wanderers we are describing them by the attempts they make. In the Christian tradition, we define human beings as ethical agents or ethical doers. We are prepared to grant sentience but not sapience to nonlinguistic creatures. They may be beings but they are not doers like us. They are neither rational nor agential. They simply are.

Perhaps God simply is. If so, as a being, God would not be the kind of moral agent we think all humans ought to be. A divine *being* would be rationally absent and morally silent. This is Job's God. Ironically, when Adam and Eve were beings they were most like this absent and transcendent God. When they tried to be what they already were they converted themselves into human doers and they converted their way of conceptualizing God into a moral and rational Doer. The difference between seeing ourselves as beings rather than doers is to see humanity in two different paradigms. As members of the human-doers paradigm, we cannot imagine what it would be like to be human *beings*. Original Sin, or Original Grace, offers to return us to a state of being, where our value and identity are not defined by the ethical or unethical actions we take. Of course, as previously alluded to, this does not mean that we should just sin so that grace may abound.

Repentance is most needed when it is least necessary.

By all reports, Jesus fares better in public opinion polls than Christianity. People of all kinds, from believers to unbelievers, have a respect for Jesus. Believers prefer a high christological Jesus as the divine Son of God and redeemer of humankind. Unbelievers prefer a Jesus who was a great teacher who died for his convictions. In between are people who differentiate between the canonical Jesus, the one portrayed in a straightforward reading of the gospels, and the historical Jesus, the kind promoted by the Jesus Seminar. In *Zero Theology*, I tend toward a playful interpretation of Jesus that mixes the canonical Jesus with the historical and heroic versions of Jesus. Remember that we are choosing to inhabit *as if* scenarios rather than belief compulsions. For this reason, the high christological view is most likely excluded but even it could be maintained if its adherents approached it as an *as if* rather than as a truth to be believed or rejected.

In my discussion of relational space, I stated that regardless of how one enters into relational space, once one inhabits it one is irrevocably caught up in the small-world interconnectivity, butterfly effects, and opportunity costs that define it. This means that even if someone were dropped into human community from outer space, that person would immediately participate in the unintended consequences and sufferings of human life. I also stated that Augustine and traditional theology's notions of Original Sin were examples of fundamental attribution error where they mistakenly attributed the problems of a system to the dispositional flaws of individuals within that system. Relational space is my correction and redirection of that error. What this means is that even if Jesus were born of a virgin, which was meant to remove the dispositional flaw diagnosed by fundamental attribution error writ large, he would still participate in the same sin and suffering as any other individual in relational space. This is not to critique Jesus per se but is meant to show that any individual node in relational space participates in the Original Sin of suffering, no matter how wonderful or pure the intent. If the dispositional flaw is not to blame for much of the social suffering experienced by humankind, then the dispositional virtue of an ethical champion need not be called upon to redeem it.

There are two ways a dispositional, ethical champion could exist, and neither believers nor unbelievers are open to them. The first way a dispositional, ethical champion could exist would be if he or she did not participate in the web of relational space. This would mean that the champion's actions would have no impact or produce no effects elsewhere in the system, which is the opposite of what one expects or wants from an ethical champion. Such a proposal would also border on the historic heresy of Docetism, which denied that Jesus was actually a human being. Such a notion is not serious enough to analyze and would be immediately rejected by everyone.

Another way an ethical champion could exist would be if he or she could control all the effects of his or her intentional and unintentional actions. Since the causal nexus in relational space also involves the intentions and actions of other individuals, such control by an ethical champion would deprive other individuals of freedom over their own decisions. In relational space, freedom to choose between options triggers necessary but insufficient conditions within which other individuals make equally necessary but insufficient decisions. If, at any point, an individual chooses not to make the necessary choice that would ultimately lead to the ethical champion's desired goal, that goal is thwarted. If the original intender is an ethical champion, no intervening node has the freedom to avoid the necessary action. As I have stated, no one in relational space has pure freedom in that no choice only causes good and never causes pain, but when an ethical champion is present, even these less pure choices are removed and people become dominos that can only behave in such a way as to complete the original ethical champion's desired goal. This option will also not be embraced by believers or unbelievers. Even the most determined determinists would not accept an ethical champion who determined everyone's actions.

It would seem then that Jesus is a sinner, just like the rest of us. He would be no more capable of avoiding Original Sin than any other person born into relational space. Jesus lived under the same conditions as the rest of us. Small-world interconnectivity and butterfly effects mean that even when Jesus raises someone from the dead, he has no way of controlling that person's future actions and the pain that will result from them. In fact, the very act of raising someone from the dead causes pain elsewhere as others ask why he will not raise their dead loved ones. Opportunity costs affect Jesus in the same way they affect anyone else. When Jesus heals the blind man on the street he is choosing not to heal the blind man on the next block. Jesus does not feed all the hungry, only those with whom he has direct encounters. This is not a moral flaw in Jesus just as it is not a moral flaw in anyone else. However, since Original Sin describes the human condition as the causing of unintended suffering, Jesus is just as much a participant in Original Sin as we are.

These complaints about the limitations of Jesus's miracles assume that he actually had the power to do them and presumes the usual supernatural intervention definition commonly held. Ignoring my previous criticism of this definition, these complaints reflect the criticisms many make against an all-powerful and loving God. "Why doesn't God heal everyone?" "Why won't God raise people today?" Theodicy tries to answer these criticisms in the same way that Job's friends did when Job was suffering. Both the critique and the defense assume that God is present and vocal in an obvious way and that God's actions stand in need of justification. Jesus is different in that he was present and active and experienced the same absent God as the rest of us. If God is immune to the kinds of criticisms raised against Jesus in this section, it is only because God does not inhabit relational space in the way that Jesus did.

There is one other way to preserve the sinlessness of Jesus, however, and it is a way that is open to each of us. I have stated that since Original Sin was not entered into through temptation, it cannot be exited through conviction. Temptation and conviction are converse synonyms. They are different terms for the same door. The Original Sin that one commits without being tempted is the social harm that one commits simply by being alive in relational space. Since simply being alive is not entered into through temptation and is therefore not considered a sin, it is not subject to moral conviction and thus never the reason one repents, unless one adopts an attitude of what I would call *absolute repentance*.

In Plato's *Apology*, Socrates describes the process he undertook when he heard that the oracle at Delphi had proclaimed that he was the wisest of all. He went to those who were purportedly wise and questioned them about their wisdom. Under Socrates's examination, however, none of the so-called wise people turned out to be very wise. After similar investigations with philosophers, artists, and artisans, Socrates comes to accept the words of the oracle. However, Socrates notes that he came to identify his wisdom in an ironic sense. He came to believe that he was wisest of all because he, more than anyone else, knew that he was not wise.[1]

I would suggest that one way of inhabiting the Jesus story is to see Jesus *as if* his sinlessness is like Socrates's wisdom. As I have shown, it is impossible for anyone to inhabit the web of relational space and not be compromised by the unintended sufferings caused within it. This would be true even if an individual always and only made decisions with the best and noblest of intentions. Just as Socrates achieved his wisdom with a kind of ironic knowledge of the things he did not know, we could say that Jesus achieved his sinlessness with a kind of ironic awareness of how much sin he participated in on a daily basis. Just as Socrates adopted a life of seeking out those wiser than himself we could say that Jesus spent a life repenting for sins he did not intentionally commit. This is absolute repentance. Absolute repentance does not repent of this or that bad action. Absolute repentance repents for all actions, even the suffering caused by occupying relational space.

Though not the goal of *ZeroTheology*, seeing Jesus's sinlessness as ironic offers a very satisfying explanation for the two events in the life of the historical Jesus that typically go unchallenged by critics. The first is the apparent historical fact that Jesus was baptized by John the Baptist. The inclusion of this story in the gospels has long puzzled New Testament scholars because it seems to have made early Christians very uncomfortable. At the very least, being baptized by John seems to place Jesus in a subordinate position to him. More troubling to early Christians, however, was the fact that John baptized for the repentance of sins. This implies that Jesus went to John so he could be baptized for his sins. If I take the historian's view, I am perfectly willing to grant that this kind of baptism happened in an unremarkable way and that Jesus got baptized like anyone else. If I take the canonical view, however, I am forced to explain Jesus's baptism in a way similar to the Gospel of John, which converted the baptism from repentance of sins to a means of identifying the coming of the new Elijah.[2]

1. See Plato, *Apology*.
2. See John 1:29–33.

I feel tied to neither the historical nor the canonical views of Jesus's baptism. I am more interested in an interpretation that makes the Jesus character more engaging with complicated, modern life. To do this, I would adopt an *as if* attitude that suggests that Jesus may have been baptized by John the Baptist, not in repentance of the sins he had committed, but in repentance of the sins he had not intentionally committed. This means more than sins of omission, of having not helped the stranger by the side of the road. This is about all the pain Jesus or any of us causes by simply relating with others in relational space. It seems to me that a powerful story of Jesus could be told where he was weighed down by the pain he could not help causing because he was uniquely aware of unintentional relational trauma and his part in causing or perpetuating it. If interpreted in this way, his miracle stories could be lifted as examples of Jesus undoing the pain he did not cause in an effort to counteract the unintended pain he did cause. This would be a religious life not based on belief or works, but a religious life based on an *as if*, where one *unworks* salvation.

The second claim about the life of Jesus that has been accepted by critical scholars is that he was crucified as a criminal by the Roman government. I imagine his execution was no more remarkable than any of the other thousands of crucifixions that occurred during that time. Traditional theology accounted for Jesus's execution by connecting his death to the sacrificial lamb used in the Jewish day of atonement. This interpretation presumed the dispositional assessment of human evil as located in the hearts or wills of individual human beings. Even though Hebrew practices from Hebrew scriptures often involved an element of seeking corporate forgiveness for unintended sins, these aspects lost significance as the concept of individualism rose in the ancient world and culminated in Enlightenment thinking. An alternate way of viewing the crucifixion would be to say that just as Jesus was baptized for sins he did not intentionally commit, he was crucified for sins he did not intentionally commit. Jesus recognized the interconnected web referenced earlier in Dr. Martin Luther King's letter from the Birmingham jail. This recognition shows itself not only in the life Jesus lived, where he unworked sufferings in relational space by healing circumstantial and absolute griefs, but also in his willingness to practice absolute repentance. This absolute repentance shows up in his baptism by John, in his teachings about forgiveness, the Lord's Prayer, and his willingness to be executed without protest.

As I have already mentioned, the crucifixion scene itself is a lesson in relational space. Each party at the crucifixion could reasonably claim to be in the right. Previously I referenced Jesus's famous quotation from Psalm 22, "My God, my God, why have you forsaken me!?" to describe the authentically human feeling of being godforsaken. Now, I would reference another last saying from Jesus, "Father, forgive them; for they do not know what they are doing."[3] This saying has been traditionally interpreted as though Jesus is saying, "Forgive them because they do not know who they are crucifying." Instead, I suggest that Jesus is saying, "Forgive humanity because they are not aware of all the pain their actions cause." Even when everyone is doing the right thing, innocent people suffer.

Repentance is a concept that only makes sense when one commits an action that one feels is morally wrong. Morally wrong actions are typically restricted to intentionally wrong actions or momentary mistakes where one violates an ethical prescription despite knowing better. This type of moral infraction is easily conceived of as the result of temptation. One is tempted to make an unethical attempt. After making the unethical attempt, one is convicted and repents. These are the circumstances that give rise to the concept of repentance and in which the word has its ordinary meaning.

Absolute repentance, on the other hand, violates the usual circumstantial requirements by demanding that one repent of all one's actions. To repent of all one's actions moves repentance out of the strictly ethical sphere and makes it a religious practice. Just as one is being religious when one feels absolutely safe, has absolute wonder, and feels absolutely grateful, one is choosing the transcendent option that is neither reasonable nor unreasonable. The ironic nature of Socrates's wisdom suggests that irony is an essential feature of absolute practices. This is because when one makes an absolute choice, one is well aware that there is no compulsion to do so and no extrinsic reward for doing so.

The innocence that comes from practicing absolute repentance is an ironic innocence, of course—the kind of innocence Jesus possessed. It is a commitment to unworking the sufferings of relational space wherever one can. One does not do this because one has to or in order to gain the favor of a divine judge; one does this because the journey is its own reward. This commitment comes as close as possible to merging ethical space with relational space and is based only on the simple and universal human experience that imposed suffering causes circumstantial grief.

3. Luke 23:34 NRSV.

In an earlier discussion about miracles, I stated that I could think of two absolute miracles in the Christian tradition, the Virgin Birth and the Resurrection of Jesus. An absolute miracle addresses absolute need rather than circumstantial needs. Most miracle stories are about meeting a circumstantial need. I have just stated that the miracle of the Virgin Birth does not get Jesus out of the tragedy of relational space that all human beings inhabit. Because I am wishing to escape the belief paradigm, I do not wish to be seen as disbelieving the miracles any more than I want to be seen as believing them. Living *as if* the Virgin Birth is an absolute miracle is one way of inhabiting a new paradigm.

The Virgin Birth, as opposed to other scriptural accounts of unexpected pregnancies from previously barren couples, is not about relieving the circumstantial grief over the inability to have a child. It is about announcing the possibility of dealing with absolute grief and offering the possibility of absolute hope. Absolute hope is impossible to acquire or generate through direct means. One can have direct circumstantial hope for food or a job or a date. One cannot have direct absolute hope because there is no visible target with which to align one's aim. Wherever one identifies a particular target and calls it absolute hope, one is actually aiming for circumstantial hope or denial. Any direct hope will be the name of a mattress. All mattresses are circumstantial hopes or impediments to confronting absolute grief.

Absolute hope is the offspring of parents who cannot have children. Those parents are acceptance and courage, two virtues not normally seen together. Because absolute hope is a conceptual impossibility, it is not something to be believed or disbelieved. The Virgin Birth is not a claim about an event that may or may not have happened in history. If one needs to believe in the Virgin Birth as a historical event in order to be religious, one is dependent on a mattress of denial. However, if one lives religiously by embodying the hope that comes from acceptance and courage, believing in it is beside the point. This is the goal of the liberated religious life.

TENTH CATCH

Forgiveness is only possible when it is impermissible.

You can only give mercy when you are justified in not giving it. If mercy is justified, then it is impossible. Mercy can only be given when there is no reason to give it. In his sermon "Loving Your Enemies," Martin Luther King Jr. said,

> When the opportunity presents itself for you to defeat your enemy, that is the time which you must not do it. There will come a time, in many instances, when the person who hates you most, the person who has misused you most, the person who has gossiped about you most, the person who has spread false rumors about you most, there will come a time when you will have an opportunity to defeat that person. It might be in terms of a recommendation for a job. It might be in terms of helping that person to make some move in life. . . . When the opportunity presents itself when you can defeat your enemy, you must not do it.[1]

There is no reason to show mercy. King's comments encapsulate the conditions that must hold before mercy can be practiced. First, only a person who has the right to condemn can practice it. An authorized judge or a wronged party may give mercy, but he or she is not obligated or expected to give it. Second, the authorized judge or wronged party must have the capacity to withhold mercy and enact judgment. A person has not practiced mercy if he could not have chosen to do otherwise. Mercy is actually a negative virtue in that it is refraining to enact judgment. This refraining

---

1. King, "Loving Your Enemies."

may be expressed as forgiving a debt, pardoning an offense, or turning the other cheek. Put another way, mercy is choosing not to balance the moral account. When the offending party is in your debt and you refuse to collect, that is mercy.

Mercy is not to be confused with compassion. Compassion may be what drives one to be merciful but compassion is not about refusing to balance the moral account. Compassion can occur in the absence of any indebtedness. Compassion is something any person can show another person in any situation. We may say that someone was compassionate when they forgave a debt and while this would not be incorrect, it is not as precise or as profound as saying that the person was merciful.

It is important that we understand this precise definition of mercy. Not because it could not be defined in any other way (it could be and often is) or because the dictionary (or this writer) is the final authority. It is important because without this precise definition the extraordinary nature of mercy will be lost, and we will pass by the term as if we already know everything there is to know about it.

Mercy is extraordinary because there is no motivation to give it. There is no emotional motivation. It feels good to exact revenge, to get payback, to balance the moral books. When someone has wronged us, it is very satisfying to wrong that person in return. To say otherwise is to tell people that they are not really feeling what they say they are feeling. If it did not feel good to get revenge, then we would not have road rage, vigilantism, and district attorneys winning elections because they have promised to crack down on criminals. One might argue that vengeance does not pay in the long run, but there is no arguing the short-term satisfaction that vengeance delivers.

There is no political motivation for mercy. Legal systems require that persons pay for the crimes they commit. Retribution is necessary. In some cases, the offending party is required to pay for damages they have caused. At the very least, they are required to pay for their crimes against society. This is done using a variety of compensatory and punitive measures. Society requires the enforcement of its laws, and part of that enforcement involves punishing offenders. Mercy may be an attractive exception to the rule when circumstances are right, but it is never the general rule.

It is precisely because there are no motivations for mercy that an act of mercy is transcendent. Real acts of mercy may move us to tears but they are as likely to leave us dumbstruck or even offended. In 2007, when the

Amish community in Nickel Mines, Pennsylvania, forgave the man who shot and killed children at the school, outsiders looked on in disbelief.[2] Some thought they were saints, but just as many found their forgiveness incomprehensible. We look upon the merciful as though they are members of a different species. The merciful inspire something like awe or shock in the way that an alien spacecraft might if it landed in the city square. We are not prepared for mercy. It is extraordinary, not ordinary. It is supernatural, not natural. It is transcendent, not reasonable. Only a person who tries to live a radically different kind of life would practice mercy. This is the liberated religious path.

In Luke 6, we find Jesus saying something that comes close to a Catch-22.[3] The transcendent love of religious living is extraordinary or non-reasonable love. It is miraculous. It is love that is given to those who do not deserve it. In fact, they deserve the opposite. They deserve hate or the withholding of mercy. Regular love is giving love or compassion to those who give love and compassion to you. To give love to those who mistreat or hate you is to practice absolute love or mercy. It is this kind of love that Jesus exhibited to his enemies and that he called his disciples to imitate. This kind of non-reasonable love is rare in the world. People like Martin Luther King, Gandhi, and Jesus are exemplars of that kind of love. Jesus is important for Christians because he practiced this kind of love despite being the New Testament version of Job. He was supposed to be righteous and undeserving of suffering, and yet he suffered all the same. His response to suffering was the liberated religious response of *Zero Theology*. Mercy, like the religious journey, does not lead to a reward, but is the reward itself. Mercy is also dangerous, however, because it threatens to undo the very fabric that binds communities together. To understand this danger, we have

2. Shapiro, "Amish Forgive School Shooter, Struggle with Grief."

3. "But I say to you that listen, love your enemies, do good to those who hate you, bless those who curse you, pray for those who abuse you. If anyone strikes you on the cheek, offer the other also; and from anyone who takes away your coat do not withhold even your shirt. Give to everyone who begs from you; and if anyone takes away your goods, do not ask for them again. Do to others as you would have them do to you. If you love those who love you, what credit is that to you? For even sinners love those who love them. If you do good to those who do good to you, what credit is that to you? For even sinners do the same. If you lend to those from whom you hope to receive, what credit is that to you? Even sinners lend to sinners, to receive as much again. But love your enemies, do good, and lend, expecting nothing in return. Your reward will be great, and you will be children of the Most High; for he is kind to the ungrateful and the wicked. Be merciful, just as your Father is merciful" (Luke 6:27–38 NRSV).

to understand judgment, because just as God's absence establishes the context that gives God's presence any meaning, judgment provides the context that makes mercy dangerous and transcendent.

Given the fact that each of us inhabits at least one community of ethical space while also inhabiting the general human community of relational space, we are also trapped between two sins. If we avoid one, we commit the other. These two sins are connected to the problems of absolutism and relativism, though they are more nuanced than those clumsy categories. I suggest that we call these two sins *making judgments* and *passing judgment*.

The first inevitable sin of living in any ethical space is the sin of judgment. That is because the "sin" is rooted in the very thing that gives a community its identity and purpose. An intentional community organizes itself around a set of privileged prescriptions that are used as criteria for membership. Wherever there are criteria, there is judgment. *Made* judgments refer to the application of agreed-upon criteria among people who share the ethical space of a community. Made judgments are the sinew of a social contract that makes communal life possible. If mercy invalidated those judgments, the community would lose cohesion. When a community punishes people for violating its laws, the punishment is usually a form of made judgment. These judgments make community life possible. Made judgments go to actions, but only to actions of individuals who are clearly regarded as insiders or participants in the ethical community.

Passed judgments are issued not against actions but against individuals or groups. An ethical community passes judgment when it declares individuals or groups outside the bounds of its ethical space. It can only pass judgment because the ethical community lacks the authority to correct outsiders' behaviors by making judgments about those behaviors. Passing judgment differs from making judgments in that passed judgments declare whatever criteria outsiders use in making their own judgments as the wrong criteria. In other words, passing judgment is a way that any particular community or ethical space defines its boundaries. If mercy invalidated this type of judgment it would destroy the conceptual context that makes mercy possible in the first place.

These boundaries define the difference between insiders and outsiders. Those inside the boundaries will have their actions subjected to made judgments where the community presumes that insiders are making the correct moral or ethical attempts. Those outside the boundaries will be subjected to passed judgments because the ethical community does not even consider outsiders to be making the correct moral or ethical attempts. When a community punishes people for civil disobedience, it is usually a form of passed judgment because the civil disobedience is regarded as a direct attack from outsiders. The fact that the civilly disobedient see themselves as insiders reflects the stretching and shifting that can occur between made and passed judgments. Civil disobedience is trying to change something about the way an ethical community interprets or applies its privileged criteria. Whether the community perceives this change as incremental or revolutionary will determine whether they make or pass judgment on the disobeyers.

Another way of expressing the difference between made and passed judgments is to say that made judgments identify mistakes and passed judgments identify wrongness.[4] For example, imagine that basic mathematical addition comprised the agreed-upon ethical criterion for a particular ethical space. The teacher's job is to train the students in addition. Upon grading quizzes, the teacher finds that Student A answered all the addition problems correctly except one. In that instance, the teacher would declare that the student had mastered the required criterion but had made a single mistake. A red mark next to the missed equation would be a made judgment.

Now suppose that Student B has managed to answer only one math problem correctly. The teacher discovers that Student B has put "10" down as the answer to all the questions and the only question that was answered "correctly" was "6+4=." In this case, the teacher would not conclude that Student B made mistakes on every problem except one. The teacher would conclude that Student B fails to grasp basic addition or is not even trying and will need to repeat the class or receive extra instruction. This would be a passed judgment. While Student A would be an insider to the addition community, Student B would be an outsider in training.

A mistake inside an ethical community is like Student A's mistaken answer to one problem. An ethical community makes judgments on the ethical failures of its members when it perceives that they are genuinely trying to live by the community's prescriptions. For example, in conservative, evangelical communities, a person who commits infidelity within heterosexual marriage may claim to have made a mistake, and the community may accept this as a reasonable claim and offer forgiveness. Such communities are less likely to see homosexual unions as a mistake and more likely to see them as misguided or wrong attempts. This is why such communities

4. Wittgenstein, *Philosophical Investigations*, 56–57.

are not impressed when outsiders argue that homosexuals in long-term faithful relationships do more honor to the institution of marriage than heterosexuals who engage in unfaithful actions that lead to divorce. From the perspective of a conservative, evangelical community, homosexual marriage is a wrong attempt and heterosexual infidelity is an unfortunate mistake. In such communities, it is irrelevant if those making wrong attempts are successful or not. In order for conservative, evangelical ethical communities to consider homosexual fidelity as a success they would have to reorient their entire way of conceiving the ethical game of marriage. For this reason, debate between alternative ethical communities is rarely over the single issue that gives rise to the debate. The debate is between the entire ethical framework of the communities.

The line between made and passed judgments is fuzzy. A community may transition from made to passed judgment when a member's actions rise to such an offensive level that they shift that member from the category of insider to the category of outsider. When this happens, a qualitative shift occurs in the judgment. When a community passes judgment on one of its members it is saying that while that member's actions are inconsistent with the shared behavioral criteria of the community and could be subjected to made judgments, the community no longer believes that the member shares its behavioral criteria and has become an outsider. This is to say that the former member is no longer attempting to play the same game as the community. The offending member will have to go to great lengths to earn the trust of the community to be restored as an insider.

Over time, communities or ethical spaces evolve so that while they make and pass judgments, situations occur that cause these judgments to shift. Made judgments patrol whatever the ethical community regards as its essence or definitive criteria. Passed judgments patrol the ethical community's boundaries and determine the community's membership. Sometimes insiders begin to apply the community's essential definition in new ways that alter that community's boundaries. This could be triggered by increasing exposure to or developing relationships with those traditionally defined as outsiders, or it could come from a reevaluation of the implications of what a community claims as its central prescription. When those within an ethical community begin calling for expanding the boundaries or loosening the centralizing essence they are known as prophetic or visionary leaders.

Prophetic or visionary leaders attempt to straddle the boundary between their ethical community and outside communities. When Jesus ate with sinners, spoke of good Samaritans, and touched lepers, he was transgressing not only his community's ethical boundaries but also their conceptual boundaries. Jesus was not against all boundaries; he was only against boundaries that violated a larger ethic than the ethical boundaries of his home community. To transgress was to widen, not obliterate, those boundaries.

I know of no prophetic or visionary leader who has not or does not rely on insider/outsider categories. In fact, to surrender those categories is to surrender one's role as a prophetic or visionary leader. This is because ethical communities and prophetic leaders inhabit ethical space, and ethical space always has narrower boundaries than relational space. Prophetic leaders want to influence or transform a portion or all of the relational space they inhabit and they want their ethical space to transform in a way that makes that possible. Judging is an important part of this process. Prophets make judgments against the hypocrisy of their ethical space. They pass judgment when they seek to create a new ethical space. Judgment then is a necessary virtue and an unavoidable sin. Everyone who wants to make the world a better place commits it.

The prophetic or visionary leader will receive both made and passed judgments from members of her ethical community. The stricter a community is regarding its essence and boundaries the more likely it is to pass judgment on a prophetic leader. The more tolerant a community is regarding its essence and boundaries the more likely it is to silence the prophetic leader by categorizing her with others who are simply "mistaken." Where boundaries are too defined, prophets are banished. Where they are too porous, prophets are lost in all the noise.

Christians frequently cite Matthew 7:1–2 as a judgment against judgment. It reads,

> Do not judge, so that you may not be judged. For with the judgment you make you will be judged, and the measure you give will be the measure you get.[5]

Progressives tend to cite this passage against what they perceive to be the overly strict essentialism of conservatives. Progressives point out that conservatism, by its very nature and own admission, is hostile to prophetic or

5. Matt 7:1–2 NRSV.

visionary leaders. They suggest that conservative Christian communities would reject the very Jesus they claim to follow. Conservatives respond by citing the passage right back at progressives. They claim that progressives are violating the command not to judge when they judge conservatism. The endless accusatory postures betray the fact that neither community has done much work on analyzing the concept of judgment. They each lack the ability to distinguish made from passed judgments. They do this because they fail to differentiate ethical space from relational space.

Almost all ethical communities desire that their privileged prescriptions become universalized. In fact, the desire to universalize may be an essential feature of any community that we would recognize as ethical. If a community did not wish to universalize their privileged prescription we would likely see it more as a private club. When ethical communities desire to universalize their privileged prescriptions, they begin to apply their own privileged prescriptions or criteria to the behaviors of everyone, even outsiders. They do this while retaining their own community's distinctive boundaries. This is why conservative Christians do not believe they are "passing" judgment on homosexuals and violating Matthew 7:1–2. Instead, they believe they are only making judgments based on the universal criteria that they think all people ought to privilege. In other words, conservative, evangelical Christian communities treat homosexuals as insiders when they are "making judgments" against them based on their privileged but "universal" criteria by which everyone should be judged, but they regard them as outsiders when it comes to including them as members who accept the privileged criteria of their ethical space. This simultaneous holding of community distinction and ethical universalization leads to phrases like "we love the sinner but not the sin." Progressives do the same thing when they argue that homophobia is wrong for everyone, not just those who subscribe to progressive ideals. I am not suggesting that this universalizing desire is wrong, only that when we fail to acknowledge that we simultaneously hold both universalizing desires and community distinctiveness it makes it very difficult for us to be honest about the nature of the judgments we make and pass.

The sin of passing judgment is that it declares those who are judged to be wrong as outsiders and cuts off the possibility of relationship with them. The ethical community may desire to be in relationship with outsiders, but only on its own terms. Made and passed judgments are based on a desire to remain connected with all the individuals who comprise the ethical community. Made judgments try to do this through correction. Passed judgments try to do this through threat. The threat is banishment from the ethical community.

I have previously described prophetic or visionary leaders as those who challenge the ethical prescriptions of a community. The prophet usually calls for reassessment of what the community regards as essential and for a redefinition of what the community regards as its boundaries. I have also said that a prophet or visionary leader does this because she straddles the boundary between insiders and outsiders and wishes to expand that boundary. As I have noted, ethical communities frequently make judgments or pass judgment against prophets or visionary leaders. Because they perceive prophets or visionary leaders as outsiders from within, ethical communities feel betrayed. This betrayal moves them to label the prophet or visionary leader as a blasphemer in an attempt to identify the prophet as one who has rejected the community's ethical prescriptions. When an ethical community accuses one of its members of severing relationship, the ethical community is threatening to sever the relationship preemptively.

Believers are frequently guilty of confusing passed judgment for made judgments. The fundamentalist version of belief takes an absolutist position toward its privileged ethical criteria and proceeds to pass judgment against anyone who does not share those criteria. Since they believe that everyone should be judged based upon their privileged ethical criteria, they see no difference between the way they judge insiders and the way they judge outsiders. This is not in keeping with their actual practices. They claim that everyone is welcome as an insider as long as they accept the privileged criteria. As they pass judgment against people they disapprove of, they believe they are only making the kind of judgments that community cohesiveness requires. They do not regard this necessary judgment-making to be a violation of Jesus's teaching in Matthew 7.

The liberated religious are more tempted to refrain from judgment because of their fear of absolutism and their reaction against fundamentalism. The progressive version of the liberated religious sometimes takes a relativistic position, which means that they lose the ability to distinguish made judgments from passed judgment. Since they are frequently sensitive to judging others by their own ethical criteria, they view all alternative communities as equally valid ethical spaces. This is to treat these other communities as outsiders and since that would mean that any judgment reached would be passed judgment against outsiders they avoid making any judgments at all. This is to ignore the circumstantial griefs that are present across communities in the thinner slices of contextual life and to ignore the common human challenge of dealing with absolute grief. Taken to an extreme, this relativistic approach declares oneself an outsider to all ethical communities because there is no ethical prescription the relativist is willing to privilege.

The interplay between made and passed judgments, the conservative tendency toward absolutism, and the progressive tendency toward relativism may be made clearer in considering a fictional world. Imagine two communities. One is comprised of Meanderthals and the other is comprised of *homo directus*. In Meanderthal culture, individuals meander when traveling from point A to point B. They have a more relaxed attitude toward time. In *homo directus* culture, individuals move as quickly and directly as possible from point A to point B. They have a very frugal attitude toward time. As outside observers of these two cultures, most of us would grant that neither culture is better than the other and that ultimately speaking, meandering is no better or worse than moving hurriedly in a straight line. When we refuse to insist that one culture is better than the other, we are refusing to pass judgment and may be criticized as relativists or praised as tolerant. Someone who insisted that one culture was superior to the other would be an absolutist because, presumably, that superior culture's practices would be grounded in some type of divine, natural, or rational foundation. That person would be criticized as intolerant.

If we move closer to the cultures and actually inhabit them, however, we discover more variety than the generalized labels of Meanderthals and *homo directus* suggest. For example, we learn that even among Meanderthals, there is the possibility of being labeled as too meandering. They are able to distinguish between those who meander more and those who meander less. In this culture, individuals who meander less may get consideration for jobs that those who meander more will not. The same is true in *homo directus* culture. Those who move more urgently may be considered for jobs that those who move less urgently will not. If we choose to engage each of these cultures, rather than simply observe them as outsiders, we develop the ability to *make* the same kinds of judgments that each culture's native inhabitants make. In other words, we develop an ability to say that certain members of each culture are industrious and certain members are lazy. We also develop the ability to flip our judgments and say that some are too hurried and some are relaxed in a healthier way.

The ability to move from passed judgments to made judgments comes when observation gives way to habitation, when outsider observers become insider participants. Inhabiting a culture teaches one to identify the more thinly sliced contexts that comprise human life within cultures and enables one to see through the thick clumsier chunks of contexts that are sometimes identified as cultural contexts. For example, as an inhabitant we learn that both Meanderthals and *homo directus* have professional ambulance drivers who transport injured people to hospitals. We learn that in both cultures, the expectation is that these ambulance drivers get the injured parties to hospitals as quickly and directly as they can. In Meanderthal culture, an ambulance driver who meanders to the hospital will lose his job. He will not lose his job because Meanderthals became convinced that *homo directus* have it right and Meanderthals have it wrong. He will be fired because the context that determines how his actions will be judged is a much thinner slice than the cultural context in which he resides. It would be possible for a joint commission of both Meanderthals and *homo directus* to establish a policy that all ambulance drivers should drive like *homo directus* because in that one very specific thin slice of life, the speedy directness of *homo directus* matches the need to get people to the hospital as quickly and directly as possible. Such a proclamation would not be passing judgment against Meanderthals; it would be making judgments about ambulance drivers. Contexts come in a variety of thicknesses, and those thicknesses often determine which criteria are to be used when assessing behaviors within them.

This imagined scenario suggests that both conservatives and progressives underestimate the power of context. Conservatives tend toward a transcontextual absolutism that is blind to the role their own context plays in forming their convictions regarding ethics. Their absolutism keeps them insisting on only one way to be a human doer. They see only one thick context when assessing human behavior. Progressives recognize contexts that are more thinly sliced than their own context but they usually stop once they discover cultural or community contexts. Their failure to recognize even thinner contexts prevents them from seeing connections across cultural contexts that create the possibility of cross-cultural relationships that require the making of judgments. Their relativism keeps them insisting that there really is no such thing as a human community and that all we have are different ethical spaces that are more or less commensurable. They commit a sociological form of fideism. By balancing the obvious truth that our cultures or ethical spaces shape and define us in ways that make us different from each other with the equally obvious truth that the thinner slices of human life shape and define us in ways that make us similar to each other, we can avoid the arrogance of absolutism that blindly passes judgment and the paralysis of relativism that prevents us from making judgments as members of a common species. Different cultures will sometimes experience circumstantial griefs more intensely than others due to the way power has been utilized by privileged cultures against less privileged cultures. That is undeniable and important. But the circumstantial griefs experienced by individuals between cultures are not so different as to preclude communication. The same may be said about our experiences of absolute grief.

The two unavoidable sins of judgment are present in any cooperative human endeavor. Made judgments make the cooperative endeavor possible but establish practices that empower and disempower the way people participate in the cooperative endeavor. This often happens in a game or organization. Made judgments can ruin the endeavor for those trying to participate. Nothing can be played if rules are so overly enforced that the game ceases to be enjoyable or meaningful. On the other hand, passed judgments, which also make cooperative endeavors possible, lead to expulsion and oppression by those who are judged as wrong. The two sins of judgment are also virtues that work to make sure there is enough definition at the core and enough flexibility at the boundary to make the community strong yet adaptable. There is no avoiding these two sins. In avoiding one of the sins, a person commits the other.

It is important to understand the distinction between made and passed judgments when we look at each kind of judgment from the perspective of Original Grace. Though Original Grace diminishes the stigma of causing pain in the interconnected web, unlike the traditional idea of grace, it does not do so by utilizing concepts having to do with forgiveness. In our legal tradition, persons found guilty of perpetrating unlawful actions may go unpunished if their actions are justified or excused. The distinction between justification and excuse mirrors the distinction between made and passed judgments.

Generally speaking, the legal concept of justification states that in some circumstances an act that is normally considered a criminal or bad act may be justified. Justification converts the criminal or bad act into a legal or good act (or at least not a bad act). Justification goes to actions. It is a made judgment. Made judgments decide whether an action is good or bad within the boundaries of an ethical community. Justification rules that an act is not bad. Sometimes, our legal system expresses justification by saying that the person or actor was justified in doing the act. This is a shorthand way of saying that the action the person performed is justified. This shorthand is misleading. The action is justified, not the actor. We know this because justification can be transferred to the actions of other actors. The traditional justification defenses include self-defense, defense of others, defense of property, civil disobedience and defense by necessity. Let us take a self-defense example from Joshua Dressler: "If X provides D with a gun used to kill V in justifiable self-defense, X is guilty of no crime."[6] If an act is justified, it does not matter who commits it. This is why justification actually goes to actions rather than individuals, despite the fact that we often shorten our descriptions to say that the person was justified. There is no need to be merciful to people whose actions have been justified because there is no harm that needs forgiveness, unless one wants to use mercy in a creative and poetic way.

Excuse defenses differ from justification defenses in that excuse goes to the actor rather than the action. When someone makes an excuse defense, the unjustifiability of the act is not contested. The person admits to performing the unjustified or bad action. However, the person wishes to be excused for performing this bad action because of extenuating circumstances. According to Dressler, "Perhaps the broadest excuse theory states that a person should not be blamed for conduct if it was caused by factors outside her control."[7] The best-known example of an excuse defense is the insanity defense. The excuse defense sounds familiar to anyone who knows the debate that occurred between Augustine and Pelagius. Pelagius suggested that if humankind lacked the capacity to perform God's commandments they should be excused rather than condemned. He suggested that Augustine made God a monster who asked more of humanity than humanity could perform. Pelagius would have been a great defense lawyer arguing for his client to be excused because he would say that it is unethical for an ethical community to judge the actions of an individual who was unable to perform those actions satisfactorily. Excuses go to the actor rather than the action, and this is revealed in the fact that excuses cannot be transferred. If person A assists person B in the performance of a bad act and person B is excused, person A will not be excused if he or she does not share person B's

---

6. Dressler, *Understanding Criminal Law,* 217.

7. Dressler, *Understanding Criminal Law,* 211.

inability to perform a lawful action. Granting an excuse is also not an act of mercy because the individual lacks the ability to incur a debt that requires forgiveness.

Before I return to Original Grace and forgiveness, I also need to discuss the roles that necessity and duress play in the justification and excuse defenses just described. Necessity is a justification defense that states, "If circumstances compel a choice among various evils an actor should not be punished if he chooses the least harmful option."[8] Defendants may make a necessity-based defense if their act occurred under imminent threat, their choice was reasonable, they had no legal alternative, their act resulted in a less serious harmful result than would have resulted from an alternative act, there are no legislative predetermining restrictions, and they did not create the harmful necessity in the first place.[9] In a necessity defense, the action is justified because, presumably, there is no other actor who could be prosecuted. Necessity reflects a creation of conditions over which no individual has control. The actions are justified because they were necessary in some way.

Duress on the other hand is an excuse defense and occurs when one individual or group coerces another individual or group to take a bad action. The elements of a duress defense typically include a threat to kill or seriously injure the actor or a third party, an actor who reasonably believed the threat to be genuine, and an immediate or impending threat.[10] In an excuse defense, the defendant claims that he or she was neither morally culpable nor legally responsible for the bad action because another party coerced the defendant into performing the bad act. In excuse defenses, it is possible to prosecute another party because there is a bad actor to which the bad action can be traced. Excuse goes to the actor, who had no control over the action.

Much theology has been written regarding the nature of human beings and how their actions may be justified or excused. Justification is a long-standing theological concept that goes back to Paul, particularly in Galatians and Romans. In Galatians, Paul has his famous dispute with Peter over Peter's refusal to eat with Gentiles. Paul writes in the famous passage,

> . . .yet we know that a person is justified not by the works of the
> law but through faith in Jesus Christ. And we have come to believe

8. Dressler, *Understanding Criminal Law*, 286.

9. Dressler, *Understanding Criminal Law*, 286–87.

10. Dressler, *Understanding Criminal Law*, 297.

in Christ Jesus, so that we might be justified by faith in Christ, and not by doing the works of the law, because no one will be justified by the works of the law.[11]

The key to justification for Paul is faith in Jesus Christ. This sounds like what *Zero Theology* might call absolute justification, in that it is no longer circumstantial actions or works, to use New Testament language, that are being justified, but the person who is being justified. I have just stated that in our legal system we sometimes use shorthand and say that an individual is justified when we really mean that the action taken by the individual is justified. Paul is not using shorthand when he speaks of those who are justified by Jesus. He is doing something more like the intentional misuse of a concept. Just as I have described the intentional misuses of safety, gratitude, and wonder, I think I can say that Paul is doing something similarly creative with justification. He takes a term that normally applies to an action and applies it to individuals. He has mixed justification with excuse.[12]

The problem for Paul is both paradigmatic and pragmatic. On the one hand, to be "under the law" is to live in a paradigm that defines righteousness by doing or making an obedient attempt. This is his paradigmatic problem. Pragmatically, his problem is, as he famously states in Romans, that "all have sinned and fallen short of the glory of God."[13] One could say that this faith in Jesus, which Paul links to his atoning death, is a paradigm shift from seeing faith as doing to seeing faith as being. In *Zero Theology*, I offer a similar recommendation. In place of belief I would put living the imaginative *as if* and making a transcendent choice in the face of absolute grief. Either way, it is about inhabiting a new way of religious living that may one day be thought of as a new paradigm.

It seems that Paul, and Augustine after him, saw divine forgiveness as something like our modern legal concept of excuse. Paul and Augustine were sure that human beings had a dispositional flaw. According to Augustine and traditional Western theology, it took Jesus, who lacked the dispositional flaw, to atone for the sins of human beings. Through Jesus, then, God could excuse humanity much in the same way that our modern

11. Gal 2:16 NRSV.

12. While I think it important to have some understanding of what Paul may or may not have meant in these early Christian documents, I do not think that the way out of the belief paradigm will come from getting back to the original Greek or understanding Paul's theology in historical context. Those kinds of studies, which I do consider valuable, are tools within the belief paradigm rather than means of escaping it.

13. Rom 3:23 NRSV.

legal system excuses someone of wrongdoing if we determine that the person lacked the mental capacity to obey the law. But Paul does not use the excuse idea; he goes with a creative misuse of justification that does not make bad acts right but makes bad actors righteous. Perhaps this creative mix of justification and excuse is a way of getting to something novel called divine forgiveness.

ZeroTheology's Original Sin/Original Grace differs from Paul and Augustine in that Original Sin is not the name of a problem in need of a solution. Grace and sin are different ways of describing the same reality. Original Sin focuses on the tragedy of the conditions of relational space. Original Grace focuses on the freedom and possibilities of living in relational space. By locating the "problem" of suffering and evil in the network rather than in individual dispositions, the excuse conception of divine forgiveness is ruled out because social pain is not the result of flawed human beings. On the other hand, justification is also ruled out because every action, regardless of how noble and well intentioned, causes beneficial and harmful consequences in relational space. Original Sin says that no action can be justified. Original Grace says that no actor can be blamed for the conditions of Original Sin. This is the curse and the blessing, the responsibility and freedom of living in relational space. Original Grace is not something that is granted to this or that action. It is not an example of circumstantial forgiveness for made judgments in ethical space. Original Grace is something extended to the whole web of relational space.

What is important to recognize is that no ethical community can excuse or forgive or justify the harmful effects made by its members elsewhere in relational space because ethical communities have narrower boundaries than relational space. That kind of excuse or forgiveness or justification could only come from a perspective that transcends all ethical communities and understands the contextual complexities of human actions in relational space. It is to see the human race in the light of stained-glass windows. Just as we make exceptions and extend grace to ourselves and our friends when we commit fundamental attribution error when judging others, this perspective would see every human being as friend. This is why grace is a gift from God. This is to say that a conceptual role God is called upon to play is to judge not just various ethical communities in ethical spaces, but the human community that occupies relational space. Since no human can occupy that trans-contextual position, it is something we expect from God. God is intimately connected with the human context or situation and that intimate connection renders God an ironic judge who always grants absolute mercy. Since only a wronged party can perform the transcendent act of showing mercy or offering forgiveness, God plays the role of every individual in relational space who is harmed in a way that cannot be traced. When harm cannot be traced and the harmful action not identified, there is no identifiable person to forgive. God stands in the complex causal connections in relational space that link victims to unknown and unknowing perpetrators and forgives those who could not be otherwise forgiven.

If God is seen as transcendent, above all ethical space and relational space, then the Christian identification of Jesus with the divine is to say that Jesus occupied the interconnected web in a way that God never could. To say that Jesus died for sins he did not commit is to say that Jesus, as a visionary leader, understood that often the limitations of a visionary leader become the limitations of an ethical community. By dying what might be called an infinite death, where he experienced all the relational pain of relational space, he opened the possibility that human beings could practice ironic or absolute repentance by standing in solidarity with human pain and seeking to unwork it. This is not a doctrinal claim. This is merely an invitation to inhabit a story *as if* this were its desired outcome.

As a liberated religious Christian, one could say that God stands in relationship to relational space in the same way that Jesus stands in relationship to ethical space. As a prophetic or visionary leader, Jesus transcends the boundaries of all ethical spaces and calls us to welcome the enemy, stranger, and neighbor by transforming our ethical essentials and boundaries. Jesus calls us to do the best human doers can do. God, on the other hand, transcends the boundaries of relational space. This is not an epistemological claim about something that exists beyond relational space. It is a statement that expresses God's absence as presence. What this transcendent God, who is morally silent and rationally absent, reminds us of is that we are human beings and that even as we try to do the best human doers can do, we need no longer be defined exclusively by the doer paradigm of moral attempt. Like Adam and Eve before the fall, we are accepted for who we are and not judged for what we do. This is Original Grace.

Because mercy or forgiveness is a transcendent act, Matthew 12:31–32 in interesting because it is where Jesus mentions that blasphemy against the Holy Spirit is unforgivable. He says it in response to Pharisees who accuse him of casting out demons using the power of Beelzebul. The Pharisees are clearly issuing a judgment when they accuse Jesus in this way. It is certainly more than a made judgment because when the Pharisees associate Jesus with Beelzebul they label him an outsider. It is a passed judgment because the Pharisees judge his criteria for what makes something good or evil. In most instances, when judging is condemned in the New Testament it is condemned despite the fact that the judgment might have some validity. The men who judge the woman caught in adultery in John 8 are not shamed because their judgment is incorrect. She is an adulterer. They are shamed for their hypocritical and selective use of judgment and by their carelessness about the contexts of her life. In this case, however, the Pharisees's judgement is of a different sort. In this case, they are attributing the healing and good work of Jesus to the harmful and evil work of Beelzebul. They are declaring Jesus an outsider from within. Jesus responds by passing judgment on the Pharisees because they are clearly outsiders to the ethical community he is trying to create, the kingdom of heaven.

In this case, it appears that the Pharisees and Jesus are playing two different ethical games employing very different ethical criteria and that both are passing judgment on the other. What each party considers good the other party considers evil. When Jesus acts in a way that challenges the ethical criteria accepted by the Pharisees, they pass judgment against him. When the Pharisees reject the ethical criteria promoted by Jesus, he passes judgment against them. Both are quitting the other party's community. To quit the community is the unforgivable sin because it passes judgment on the entire ethical criteria of a community and renders continuing relationship impossible. The reason it is called blasphemy against the Holy Spirit may be because the Spirit works to create community rather than division. At least that is how Pentecost, the advent of the Holy Spirit, is typically interpreted.[14]

What each party is doing in this passing of judgment is defining what kind of community each wants to have. This is absolutely necessary. A prophetic or visionary leader is not calling for an undefined community. A prophetic or visionary leader is calling for a differently defined community. In this regard, conservative believers understand something that progressive believers do not. Where conservative believers go wrong is in their assumption that boundaries should never be expanded or challenged. Where progressive believers go wrong is in their assumption that boundaries are always exclusionary in an unjust way. In extreme form, this type of progressivism adopts relativism. As previously stated, relativism is a position that

14. Acts 2:1–21.

is noncommittal to any ethical prescriptions, and as such it is the ultimate blasphemy against the Holy Spirit, because it refuses to belong anywhere.

Nathaniel Hawthorne wrote of the unforgivable sin of blasphemy in his short story "Ethan Brand." In it, the former lime burner had spent eighteen years searching for the Unpardonable Sin and had returned to his former lime kiln on Mount Graylock. Ethan's return to the kiln was the cause of much excitement as townsfolk came out to see the man who had searched for the great sin. Ethan Brand was so disgusted by the shabby, drunken habits of the locals that he began to doubt that he had found the sin after all. It was not until he recalled how he had destroyed the life of a girl named Esther that he reminded himself that he had in fact found the sin. In the story, it seems clear that the Unpardonable Sin has to do with outgrowing the need for human connection. It is almost as though Brand sees human beings as playthings meant for his experimentation. Ethan Brand was prone to commit the Unpardonable Sin because he was thoughtful, and his thoughts led him to pursue something other than human companionship. When Bartram, the current lime burner, asks Ethan Brand to define the unpardonable sin, Brand says, "The sin of an intellect that triumphed over the sense of brotherhood with man, and reverence for God, and sacrificed everything to his own mighty claims."[15] We are told that Brand's pursuit of intellect had so broken his connection with others that "he had lost his hold of the magnetic chain of humanity."[16] When he threw himself into the lime kiln and his flesh burned away, his heart was found to be of marble.

I bring up the story of Ethan Brand because it is as if he has stopped playing the one game that human beings are not permitted to abandon. He has stopped trying to play the morality or ethical game. He has so separated himself from community and context that he has achieved the status of an amoral being. He no longer makes any ethical attempt. He is above both love and hate. He has abandoned the doing of any ethical criteria and returned to being. I think this is why his momentary disgust at the townsfolk made him temporarily doubt that he had committed the Unpardonable Sin. Anyone who had committed it would be beyond moral disgust. When he recalled how he had played with the girl Ester he was reassured that he had in fact committed it. If Ethan Brand did not inhabit a moral world, he would not be that different from Adam and Eve in Eden. Amorality is as close as

15. Hawthorne, "Ethan Brand," 427–28.
16. Hawthorne, "Ethan Brand," 436.

one can come to premorality. There is therefore a connection between the Unpardonable Sin and the conditions of Original Sin. What they share is that neither sin is governed by the usual ethical or moral rules. When an individual passes judgment on an ethical community and declares himself an outsider to that community, that individual has committed that community's unforgivable sin—not because the community would not restore that individual, provided he recants, but because he will not recant, the community cannot restore. In Ethan Brand's case, he has rejected the criteria of all ethical communities and has become an amoral relativist. Interestingly enough, those prone to becoming prophetic or visionary leaders are most vulnerable to this unforgivable sin. Because visionary leadership requires transcending the ethical criteria of one's native community, it can sometimes turn into a feeling of transcendence over all ethical spaces.

If we attempt to undo the fall of Adam and Eve by returning to being and forsake doing we turn our back on the interconnected web and the effect we have on one another. If we become beings only, we commit Ethan Brand's Unpardonable Sin and commit the blasphemy of separating ourselves from the ethical game of humanity. This ethical game is the game that all human doers are expected to play. The profound message of Original Sin/Original Grace is that while we are expected to be doers, or at least moral attempters, we are not going to be held responsible for our actions. This knowledge frees human beings to act not based on fear of judgment or promise of reward, but out of a general sense of being, which is to go on a journey that is its own reward, to feel absolutely safe, absolutely grateful, absolutely wondrous, and absolutely merciful.

Conclusion and Resurrection?

This is the famous image known as the "duck/rabbit." Some see a duck and then have to go looking for the rabbit. Others see the rabbit and have to go looking for the duck. The "duck/rabbit" has been around since the late 1800s, but Ludwig Wittgenstein used it to talk about the difference between interpretation, or *seeing as*, and the non-interpretive direct encounter.[1] Thomas Kuhn used it as an example of a paradigm shift.[2]

Suppose there was a culture where no one had ever seen a rabbit. Members of that culture would only see a duck when looking at the "duck/rabbit." They would not see the image *as* a duck. They would see a duck, much like English speakers do not see an *F as* an F. They just see F. That is the natural and direct way English speakers encounter F. You would only have to interpret the mark *as an F* if another way of seeing that mark was available to you. In the same way, a culture that only knew rabbits and knew nothing of ducks would only see a rabbit and would not do so as an interpretive act. We who know and see both ducks and rabbits would say of these single-perception cultures that the people are sincere. The people in

1. Wittgenstein, *Philosophical Investigations*, 194–213.

2. Kuhn, *Structure of Scientific Revolutions*, 111–35.

that culture would not describe themselves that way because sincerity only enters the picture when the picture can be doubted or interpreted.

In a culture where people know both ducks and rabbits there would be the possibility of interpretation. Not all of them would exercise that possibility. It is quite possible to know all about rabbits and only see a duck when looking at the image. But once someone showed you the rabbit, then you would have the possibility of interpretation. If one writes the word "quack" above the image one can guide onlookers to interpret the image as a duck. If one writes, "what's up doc?" above the image one can guide onlookers to interpret the image as a rabbit. You may always see one of the images first and then have to interpret the other image in order to see it. Nevertheless, those who have seen both a duck and a rabbit encounter the image in a different way than those who have always and only seen the image as a duck or a rabbit.

There may have been a time in Western history when we could say that Christians knew of only one religious option. In our analogy, we could say they always and only saw a duck. We could say that their conceptual options were limited. People could have still had doubts or failed to live up to their religious ideals but not because they could imagine seeing the world in a different or nonreligious way. As such, we could say that such people were conceptually, if not practically, as incapable of sincerity as they were of duplicity. But after the Enlightenment, more and more people began to realize that another option of seeing the world was available. Plenty of people continue to see only a duck, but they are aware that others see something different. Once this awareness of different perspectives becomes possible, it becomes possible to speak of sincerity and duplicity. The sincere believer, after the Enlightenment, is aware that there is a rabbit, but can only make sense of the duck. If someone can only see a duck in a world where people also see rabbits, we can say that the person has a sincere belief about what it is the image depicts. *Belief* stands and falls with *interpret* and *sincere*, because it only becomes possible once the possibility of doubt has been raised. Before the possibility of doubt, what we now call belief was a part of the paradigmatic bedrock of ideas that people took for granted. The belief paradigm fails to recognize this when it looks back through history to a time before the Enlightenment. This is like people looking back to a time before transparent glass and assuming that early people thought that colored glass was flawed.

On numerous occasions, I have indicated that when one makes a straightforward religious claim about the world, a nonreligious claim or explanation must be available if the conditions of religious living are to be present. Another way of saying this would be to say that for every religious duck, there must be a nonreligious rabbit. When believers make miraculous religious claims about something, they are often arguing that the only correct way to see the world is to see it as a duck. Unbelievers, on the other hand, argue that the only correct way to see the world is to see it as a rabbit. We could say that both parties are trapped by the belief paradigm and that their opposing interpretations are built into the constituent parts of the paradigm itself. If belief, particularly sincere belief, is the standard for what counts, then one either believes sincerely or does not. The belief paradigm offers no middle ground.

What is clear is that the image is the same whether one sees a duck or a rabbit. The ability to move from seeing it as one or the other and then seeing it change does not involve any change to the image itself. A person who knows nothing of ducks or rabbits would trace the same image as those who are convinced that it is one or the other. Returning to the two cultures who always and only see the image as either a duck or a rabbit, we could say that the two cultures are living in different paradigms. If taken in this way, the "duck/rabbit" can be used as Kuhn used it, as an example of paradigms, and we could start a conversation on what it would take to get either or both cultures to shift. However, when we begin seeing the difference between *seeing the image as* a duck or *as* a rabbit, we are having an intra-paradigmatic conversation rather than an inter-paradigmatic conversation. Where two or more interpretations become possible within a culture, and members of that culture can see the possibility of these differing interpretations, we are not talking about differing paradigms. Because a paradigm determines how interpretations are made or judged and what evidence or criteria are used, one cannot occupy a trans-paradigmatic perspective from which one can independently judge one paradigm by another.

This is not to say that a newly formed paradigm cannot absorb, explain, and use the concepts formed in a previous paradigm. Einsteinian physicists are perfectly capable of understanding and using Newtonian physics without losing the distinction between the two and without surrendering why Einsteinian physics helps explain some things that Newtonian physics cannot. To put it another way, if a culture only saw ducks they could gradually acquire the ability to see rabbits and still remember what it was like when they could only see ducks, though they could never unsee the rabbit. Once this ability to distinguish paradigms arises within a culture, the dominant paradigm is able to interpret the former paradigm. This move to interpretation means that we are no longer talking about two paradigms, except in an historical sense.

This matters in *ZeroTheology* because I am trying to break out of the belief paradigm where people are divided into believers and unbelievers (or sheep and goats, or ducks and rabbits). I have already suggested that believers and unbelievers are both trapped in the same belief paradigm and I have suggested that the liberated religious perspective is a way out. It appears that I have identified two paradigms: the current belief-centered one, and a new *as if*-centered one. While it is certainly possible that culture could develop in such a way as to make these two separate paradigms, I do not think that is the case at present. Though conversation is difficult and we have to be very attentive to how we use words, we are talking about different ways of interpreting the world, not living in two separate worlds.

Because of this, the best I can suggest is that the *as if* paradigm I have been proposing is an example of one way the belief paradigm can be transcended. This is to say that in a post-belief paradigm, faith ceases to be about faith. *Faith* belongs to a conceptual cluster that involves the notions of belief and sincerity. If we could imagine a religion without sincere belief we would also imagine a religion without faith. To imagine a religion without faith is extremely difficult under the conditions of the belief paradigm. When believers and unbelievers hear about a religion without faith it sounds like no religion at all. They both interpret it in the same way. The liberated religious would not be upset with the idea of a religion without faith, which is why I call them the liberated religious rather than the faithful. I could say that they are religious but not believers. Unfortunately, the current belief-centered paradigm forces us to see *nonbelief* as *disbelief* rather than as something new or different. The current paradigm says that if it looks like a religion and quacks like a religion, it is a religion. If it does not look and quack like a religion, it is not. The contemporary conversations about the spiritual but not religious, the growth of nonreligious attitudes, and the decline of mainline Christianity are being had by ducks quacking at each other. *ZeroTheology* tries to offer something new, but the alternative it offers is not the unbelievers's rabbit, it is something else altogether.

The liberated religious continue to find meaning in religious concepts but do not look to those religious concepts for explanations about the world.

They do not see religious concepts as ideas to be believed or doubted. They are honest enough with themselves and others to admit that they experience grief for not being believers or unbelievers. They are tempted by each alternative and yet defined by the tension that both alternatives create. This tension forces them to define a new religious path. This new religious path is the most rewarding path because it is also the most difficult and most fragile. The reward is not something that comes from an external source at the end of the journey but is one that is lived during the journey, not despite obstacles, but because of obstacles.

From the perspective of unbelievers and the liberated religious, the sincerity of believers looks like denial because in order to avoid the possibility of confronting absolute grief, they have to constantly protect the beliefs that offer escape. This makes for high-anxiety living and defensiveness. Believers must discredit or deny alternative information that calls their beliefs into question. The unwillingness to critique or challenge a belief is the definition of idolatry. Believers simply want to act and trust because these are the hallmarks of their faith. Believers regard Abraham as the exemplar of faith because he acted and trusted when God told him to leave his home and go to a land he did not know.[3] For believers, sincere faith is characterized by obedience. To obey, one must sincerely believe in a divinely present authority. Abraham's two paradigmatic stories both involve obedience—the call to leave his homeland and the call to sacrifice his son, Isaac.[4] Sincere belief makes all that is positive (great commitment) and negative (willingness to use violence) about Abraham's obedience possible. Generally, but not always—because belief and obedience define what is ethical rather than empathy or connection with others—believers tend toward focusing on how their belief helps them avoid absolute grief rather than how it helps them heal the circumstantial griefs in the world. They have an easier time with loving God than they do with loving neighbor.

From the perspective of believers and the liberated religious, unbelievers seem careless or carefree in their disregard for traditional beliefs. Believers think this is terrible. The liberated religious think it enviable. Unbelievers place their trust in reason and experience. They are capable of making great ethical efforts to alleviate circumstantial grief in the world. They are better at loving neighbor and have no interest in loving God. Unbelievers are more likely to confront the worst-case scenarios associated

3. Gen 12:1.

4. Gen 22.

with absolute grief. Those who choose reasonable but alternative paths deal with absolute grief in idiosyncratic ways and do not think of those ways as religious.

The liberated religious recognize that there are no trustworthy foundational claims that can be believed. They grieve this loss even as they seek to transcend it. They are torn between their desire for the comforting beliefs of sincere believers and their desire for the freedom of unbelievers. This is what makes the liberated religious path difficult. Believers and unbelievers offer competing viewpoints about how to handle the human predicament. They understand each other, and their disagreement is over a mutually agreed-upon criterion. Believers are on guard lest their members succumb to the temptation of unbelievers' freedom. Unbelievers are on guard lest their members succumb to believers' comforting beliefs. Neither knows what to do with the liberated religious. Believers regard the liberated religious as hypocrites who are really unbelievers in disguise. Unbelievers regard the liberated religious as cowards who are really still believers but are too embarrassed to admit it. Unlike believers and unbelievers who only see each other as opposite alternatives, the liberated religious recognize both of the other options and are tempted by both sides.

The temptations of belief and disbelief offer the liberated religious the promise of relief. The sincerity of believers would relieve the liberated religious of their doubt. The freedom of unbelievers would relieve the liberated religious of the responsibility they feel for the poetic tragedy they see as the human condition. Either option offers relief from the tension that both temptations create together.

In a metaphor that might prove enlightening, Wittgenstein uses the image of the tightrope walker:

> An honest religious thinker is like a tightrope walker. He almost looks as though he were walking on nothing but air. His support is the slenderest imaginable. And yet it really is possible to walk on it.[5]

Interpreters typically take these sentences to be one of the places where Wittgenstein implies that religious belief does not need to rest upon foundations or justifications. In *ZeroTheology* I am promoting the idea that theology should have zero mattresses that help people avoid an honest confrontation with absolute grief. These mattresses are the foundations or

---

5. Wittgenstein, *Culture and Value*, 73.

justifications for religious belief. In fact, I believe these foundations or justifications get in the way of rather than support religious living. However, I would like to stretch the tightrope metaphor a little further and suggest that the liberated religious thinker is someone who is constantly having to adjust between the pull of belief on one side and the pull of unbelief on the other.

Imagine a tightrope walker holding a pole that helps her maintain balance. On one end of the pole would be belief or its defining characteristic, sincerity. On the opposite end of the pole would be unbelief or its defining characteristic, freedom. The liberated religious person finds herself frequently tempted by the sincerity of believers. Life would seem simpler if one could inhabit beliefs that help you deny the possibility of absolute grief. At the same time, the liberated religious person is tempted by the freedom of unbelievers. Life would seem easier if one could be free from having to stay on the never-ending tightrope of living a religious life that offers no comforting destination. The liberated religious are tempted by each side. The temptation is powerful because the liberated religious person knows that her only reward is the promise of life on the rope. She will not be compensated by a divinely present God for resisting the rewards offered by belief or disbelief.

The only reason for staying on the tightrope is that walking the tightrope offers a reward unavailable to believers or unbelievers. To be sure, each of those options offers rewards that are unique to each as well. Belief offers certainty that wards off absolute grief. Unbelief offers release from mandated responsibility. Believers and unbelievers are only tempted by each other because they cannot see the liberated religious tightrope. It is too thin to be perceived from their perspective. This is the tightrope walk of the liberated religious. The exemplar of the liberated religious is Job, who chose to live the religious life even when all of his reasons or motivations for doing so were lost, and yet he did not curse God.

I spend this time talking about the difference between those who live in the belief paradigm and those who try not to because it is important to understand how difficult it is to move from one paradigm to another. However, as the new paradigm develops, it will look very strange to those of us who are still trapped in the belief paradigm. There is no way to make it familiar or comfortable. There is also no way to strategize for it. The only thing we can do is try to escape the belief paradigm without knowing what religious life will look like on the other side. Awakening in a new post-belief paradigm may be to experience resurrection. When we choose the liberated religious path, the transcendent life is a foretaste of how life may be in a new paradigm.

The clearest example of a Catch-22 from Jesus is probably this: "If any want to become my followers, let them deny themselves and take up their cross and follow me. For those who want to save their life will lose it, and those who lose their life for my sake will find it."[6] I believe that Jesus is describing something very much like the subtraction of all the denials we use to avoid the confrontation with absolute grief. To say that one must give up life in order to save it is to say that one must descend down to *zero living* in order to live transcendently. There is no external reward for making the descent so there are no compelling reasons that are persuasive prior to making the descent. The reward comes only to those who choose the path of *zero living*. It cannot be evaluated theoretically prior to taking the plunge.

In this passage, the cross stands for the confrontation with and ultimate transcendence of absolute grief. It is a dark and painful process. It is not a prosperity or feel-good gospel. The reward or life gained from taking up the cross is the same as Job's reward for giving up his moral conception of God. I do not refer to the ending of Job where he gained a new family and new possessions. I refer to the wisdom and freedom he gained when his religious life was no longer built upon circumstantial mattresses.

Though sometimes interpreted as an instrumentalist command, where Jesus says if you want to gain life you have to lose it, I believe his teaching is like the seeking and finding that I covered in the First Catch. To give up your life is to gain it. It is not two separate steps. The losing is the gaining. It means that when we give up our connection to denial and our need to avoid absolute grief, we gain the freedom that comes from an honest encounter with it. This is an absolute promise, not a circumstantial guarantee. To say that when one gives up one's life for the gospel, as opposed to giving up one's life for a country, is to say that one is not placing one's trust or investing one's meaning in any other comforting mattresses of denial. To give up one's life is transcendent. To die for one's country is circumstantially noble, but religious transcendence knows no nationality. This transcendent choice to confront absolute grief is nothing less than a personal paradigm shift or conversion. To say that this personal paradigm shift is a conversion is to say that it is Easter. Transcending the belief paradigm's reasonable/

6. Matt 16:24–25 NRSV.

unreasonable addiction is to be resurrected into a life that the belief paradigm cannot imagine.

In *The Structure of Scientific Revolutions*, Thomas Kuhn says that when a paradigm is in crisis and people are torn between continuing to use the current paradigm despite its weakness or a new paradigm despite its untested status, the weight of evidence will be equal at best but will most likely favor the current paradigm. In these early stages, where the evidence favors the current paradigm, Kuhn suggests that early adopters of the untested new paradigm do so as an act of faith.[7] His use of a religious term is striking. While he was speaking of scientific revolutions, his words apply equally well (or perhaps even better) to religious revolutions. The very concept of Easter is revolution. There is no reason to believe it. There is no evidence for it. I am not saying that Easter is something that should be believed in, as the belief paradigm would insist. I am only suggesting that, conceptually, Easter stands for the kind of surprising transformation that cannot be predicted or strategically brought about. This means giving up the idea that Easter is an event that occurred in history or a result that is guaranteed if we follow certain directions. In fact, in order to experience the next Easter, we have to leave the previous Easter behind. Leaving the previous Easter behind is transgressing a boundary that the belief paradigm cannot tolerate. Those inside the belief paradigm will pass judgment on any who venture beyond the paradigm's limitations.

To live the Easter paradigm, as opposed to believing or disbelieving it, is one of the most difficult things a person can do. In the United Methodist *Book of Worship* there is a line from a prayer in the *Service of Death and Resurrection* worship order that says, "Help us to live as those who are prepared to die."[8] I take this to mean that we would like to live without fear of death and without the things we usually cling to in order to deny or avoid the reality of death. To do this would mean living without attachment to the mattresses that shield us from the pea of absolute grief. I have heard of people who have been able to live this way. I think of people like Jesus, the Buddha, Martin Luther King, and Simone Weil. I am not among them, not yet, maybe not ever. But it is the only religious life I wish to live and the only peace that passes understanding.

The Resurrection of Jesus is the other miracle that I have placed in the absolute miracle category. As opposed to the raising of Lazarus (John 11)

7. Kuhn, *Structure of Scientific Revolutions*, 157–58.
8. *The United Methodist Book of Worship*, 142.

or the twelve-year-old girl (Mark 5), it is not about relieving the circum-stantial grief of a lost loved one, but about the possibility of confronting the existential angst over mortality with the possibility of absolute peace. Circumstantial peace relies on the possibility of escaping death. Absolute peace is the peace that confronts and even blesses the role death plays in our lives. It is about fulfilling the Catch-22 Jesus gave his disciples: you can only gain life by giving it up. This is not a claim about the world that forces people to believe or disbelieve. It is a way of living the path of the liberated religious life. It is a teaching meant only for the living.

I have done all I can to bring you into a new sanctuary lit only by stained-glass windows. It is my hope that this different light will cause you to look at humanity and religious life differently. My attack on the belief para-digm and the framing religious propositions that undergird it is my attempt to show you that the bright light of science turns religion into something very unreligious. We do not notice that it has done this because we inhabit a world where clear-glass windows are the norm. I have used scriptures in new and unusual ways that do not play by the interpretive rules of the belief paradigm. This is not to say that they have been plucked from their contexts in order to make them say anything; it is to suggest a whole different light in which to read them in their contexts. The traditional interpretation pro-motes the belief paradigm. The interpretation I offer does not. I have used Catch-22s in the hope that you will be unable to know what believing or disbelieving them means. I have tried to flip you out of the belief paradigm and into something new. I have attempted to make *ZeroTheology* power-ful by using the worst-case scenario as our *as if*. This confrontation and ultimate acceptance of absolute grief is a profound experience. I have not argued that nonreligious or unbelieving people should become Christians. That would be suggesting that they should want or need it. I am suggesting that Christianity can, if seen in a different light than the belief paradigm promotes, be a way toward wisdom, courage, and love.

Stained glass is not like Augustine's stain on the human soul. There is nothing wrong with us that psychology, sociology, economics, game theory, and ethics cannot or will not explain. Like stained-glass windows, we are beautiful. We are beautiful because of our brokenness and our capacity to transcend that brokenness. Seeing humanity in the light of stained glass is not like looking at the world through rose-colored glasses. We see the ugliness, weakness, violence, and pettiness. We understand that the human story is a tragedy that offers no hope of a perfect heaven on earth or even a perfect heaven in heaven. We get it. We risk the despair that seeing these limitations might bring. But the liberated religious also see these limitations as the very conditions that make transcendent, religious life possible. We transcend these limitations with absolute courage, absolute wonder, absolute gratitude, and absolute love. We try to heal as many circumstantial griefs as we can. We look to connect with one another in intentional ways and see the possibility of absolute grief in each other's eyes. We embrace the power of the clear-glass scientific paradigm to address the circumstantial needs of our planet, but we live in the beautiful and tragic light of stained glass that shows who we are and who we can be as we struggle with absolute grief. In that light, we are beautiful, interconnected, limited, but potentially transcendent. In that light, we may respond like a statue of Mary crying for the sins of the world or like a visionary prophet who transcended the reasonable justifications of those around him and prayed, "Forgive them, they do not know what they are doing" to an absent and silent God.

Bibliography

Augustine. *The City of God*. Translated by Marcus Dods. New York: Modern Library, 2000.

Barabási, Albert-László. *Linked: How Everything Is Connected to Everything Else and What It Means for Business, Science, and Everyday Life*. New York: Penguin, 2003.

Brisac, Catherine. *A Thousand Years of Stained Glass*. Edison, NJ: Chartwell, 2001.

Descartes, René. *Meditations Concerning First Philosophy*. In *Philosophical Essays*, translated by Laurence J. Lafleur, 61–126. New York: Macmillan, 1989.

Dickens, Charles. *A Christmas Carol*. New York: Hodder & Stoughton, 1911.

Dressler, Joshua. *Understanding Criminal Law*. New York: LEXIS, 2001.

Hawthorne, Nathaniel. "Ethan Brand." In *Hawthorne: Selected Tales and Sketches*, 421–39. New York: Penguin, 1987.

Heller, Joseph. *Catch-22*. New York: Simon & Schuster, 1961.

Hopkins, Samuel. *The System of Doctrines, Contained in Divine Revelation, Explained and Defended*. 2 vols. Boston: Printed by Isaiah Thomas and Ebeneezer T. Andrews, 1793.

Houser, Nathan, and Christian Kloesel, eds. *The Essential Peirce: Selected Philosophical Writings*. Vol. 1, *1867–1893*. Bloomington: Indiana University Press, 1992.

Hume, David. *An Enquiry Concerning Human Understanding*. Amherst, NY: Prometheus, 1988.

James, William. *Pragmatism and The Meaning of Truth*. Cambridge: Harvard University Press, 1975.

Juel, Donald H. *Mark*. Minneapolis: Augsburg, 1990.

King, Martin Luther, Jr. "Letter From a Birmingham Jail." Birmingham, Alabama, April 16, 1963. The Martin Luther King Jr. Research and Education Institute, King Papers, Stanford University. https://kinginstitute.stanford.edu/king-papers/documents/letter-birmingham-jail.

———. "Loving Your Enemies." Sermon Delivered at Dexter Avenue Baptist Church, Montgomery, Alabama, November 17, 1957. The Martin Luther King Jr. Research and Education Institute, King Papers, Stanford University. https://kinginstitute.stanford.edu/king-papers/documents/loving-your-enemies-sermon-delivered-dexter-avenue-baptist-church.

Kuhn, Thomas. *The Structure of Scientific Revolutions*. Chicago: University of Chicago Press, 1962.

Macfarlane, Alan, and Gerry Martin. *Glass: A World History*. Chicago: University of Chicago Press, 2002.

Maslow, Abraham. *Motivation and Personality*. New York: Harper & Row, 1954.

Motter, Adilson, and David Campbell. "Chaos at Fifty." *Physics Today* 66 (May 2013). https://doi.org/10.1063/PT.3.1977.

Naifeh, Steven, and Gregory White Smith. *Van Gogh: The Life.* New York: Random House, 2012.

Phillips, D. Z. *The Problem of Evil & the Problem of God.* Minneapolis: Fortress, 2005.

Plato. *Apology.* In *The Last Days of Socrates,* translated by Hugh Tredennick and Harold Tarrant, 37–67. London: Penguin, 1954.

Shapiro, Joseph. "Amish Forgive School Shooter, Struggle with Grief." National Public Radio, October 2, 2007, as heard on *All Things Considered.* https://www.npr.org/templates/story/story.php?storyId=14900930.

Stanislavksy, Constantin. *An Actor Prepares.* New York: Routledge, 1936.

The United Methodist Book of Worship. Nashville: The United Methodist Publishing House, 1992.

Wittgenstein, Ludwig. *Culture and Value.* Translated by Peter Winch. Chicago: University of Chicago Press, 1980.

———. *Lecture on Ethics.* Chichester, UK: Wiley, 2014.

———. *On Certainty.* Translated by Denis Paul and G. E. M. Ambscombe. New York: Harper & Row, 1969.

———. *Philosophical Investigations.* Translated by G. E. M. Ambscombe. New York: Macmillan, 1958.

———. *Tractatus Logico-Philosophicus.* Translated by D. F. Pears and B. F. McGuiness. London: Routledge, 1922.

Index

Index

CPSIA information can be obtained
at www.ICGtesting.com
Printed in the USA
FSHW012001300919
62561FS